Author's Note

Effective business people have fine-tuned leadership and management ability backed up by exceptional decision-making, communication and creative skills and the know-how to implement it all successfully. These six areas are the basis of the 100 Greatest series.

None of these skills stands alone, each is interconnected, and for that reason I've revisited key ideas across the series. If you read more than one book, as I hope you will, you'll meet key ideas more than once. These are the framework on which the series hang and the repetition will help you become a master of modern business.

Likewise, if you only read one book, the inclusion of key ideas from across the series means that you'll benefit from seeing your chosen subject within the wider context of Leadership and Management excellence.

Good luck on your journey to becoming an effective manager within your organization.

John Adair

Contents

100 Greatest Ideas ... in an instant!

Whether you're a first time manager or an experienced leader, running a small team or an entire organization, straightforward, practical advice is hard to find.

John Adair's 100 Greatest Ideas ... are the building blocks for an amazing career, putting essential business skills and must-have thinking at your fingertips.

The ideas are short, punchy and clustered around themes, so you'll find answers to all your questions quickly and easily. Everything you need to be simply brilliant is here, and it's yours in an instant.

Look out for these at-a-glance features:

Personal Mantra –
Powerful statements as a source for inspiration

Ask Yourself –
Questions to get you thinking about the most information

Remind Yourself –
Key points to help you reflect on the Ideas

Checklist –

A list of questions to help you put the Ideas into practice

100 Greatest Ideas ... 6 Great Books

John Adair's 100 Greatest Ideas for Effective Leadership

John Adair's 100 Greatest Ideas for Personal Success

John Adair's 100 Greatest Ideas for Brilliant Communication

John Adair's 100 Greatest Ideas for Smart Decision Making

John Adair's 100 Greatest Ideas for Amazing Creativity

John Adair's 100 Greatest Ideas for Being a Brilliant Manager

JOHN ADAIR'S

100

GREATEST

IDEAS

FOR PERSONAL SUCCESS

CAPSTONE

This edition first published 2011
© 2011 John Adair

Registered office
Capstone Publishing Ltd. (A Wiley Company), The Atrium, Southern Gate, Chichester,
West Sussex, PO19 8SQ, United Kingdom

For details of our global editorial offices, for customer services and for information
about how to apply for permission to reuse the copyright material in this book
please see our website at www.wiley.com.

Wiley also publishes its books in a variety of electronic formats. Some content that
appears in print may not be available in electronic books.

Designations used by companies to distinguish their products are often claimed as
trademarks. All brand names and product names used in this book are trade names,
service marks, trademarks or registered trademarks of their respective owners. The
publisher is not associated with any product or vendor mentioned in this book. This
publication is designed to provide accurate and authoritative information in regard
to the subject matter covered. It is sold on the understanding that the publisher is
not engaged in rendering professional services. If professional advice or other
expert assistance is required, the services of a competent professional should be
sought.

Library of Congress Cataloguing-in-Publication Data

Adair, John Eric, 1934– author.
  John Adair's 100 Greatest Ideas for Personal Success / Mr. John Adair.
       p. cm
  Includes index.
  ISBN 978-0-85708-135-3 (pbk.)
   1. Creative thinking.   2. Success.   I. Title.   II. Title: John Adair's Hundred
Greatest Ideas for Personal Success.   III. Title: 100 Greatest Ideas for Personal
Success.   IV. Title: Hundred Greatest Ideas for Personal Success.
  BF408.A288 2011
  650.1–dc22

                                    2010049608

9780857081353 (paperback), 9780857081407 (epub),
9780857081414 (emobi), 9780857081582 (ebook)

A catalogue record for this book is available from the British Library.

Set in 10 on 13 pt Calibri by Toppan Best-set Premedia Limited

Printed in the United Kingdom by TJ International, Padstow, Cornwall.

Preface

Welcome to the *100 Greatest Ideas for Personal Success*.

The basic units of the book are the Ideas, which are grouped together under themes and also divided into five Parts.

As you will see, the Ideas vary considerably. Some consist of just one simple idea. Others are more like 'cluster bombs': smaller ideas about an important element. Whatever their size or shape, they all have relevance to your journey of personal success.

I am assuming that personal success matters to you. My hope is that you will find in these pages some well-tested practical guidance that will lead you in your desired direction, for personal success is an adventure.

You can imagine the Ideas as being like spokes on a wheel or pieces of amber hung on a necklace. There is no need to start reading at the beginning and go through to the end. Pick an Idea that interests you and then follow your own line of interest, so that you find what you need. As the Chinese saying goes:

> Listen to all, pluck a feather from every passing goose, but follow no-one absolutely.

You are very much in charge. May you find this book not only a handbook of practical guidance but also a source of encouragement and inspiration.

John Adair

PART ONE

Getting Your Act Together

Part One offers you some ideas on the theme of finding the work you love to do, a necessary condition, I believe, for any real measure of personal success. For it is the key to excellence. As a Japanese proverb says,

> *No man will find the best way to a thing unless he loves to do that thing.*

Common sense, isn't it? But what is common sense isn't always common practice, and what sounds simple is seldom easy.

The quest for your true role in life has an important by-product. It evokes and develops some personal qualities that you are going to find useful later on. These qualities are generic, in the sense that most successful people have them in some degree. See if you can think of any exceptions. Part One concludes with an indicative list of eight such qualities. You will notice that all of them contribute to your ability to get the best out of other people.

Within every occupational field of work there is a 'human side of enterprise'. In other words, whatever your professional or technical expertise, you need to be able to get on with people. Part One introduces this theme, one that runs throughout the book.

The greatest qualities are those which are useful to other persons.

Aristotle

Fifteen Greatest Ideas for Finding the Work You Love

Idea 1: Finding your role

I am persuaded that every being has their part to play in earth: to be exact, their own part which resembles no other.

André Gide

There is an overwhelming consensus of opinion among those who have thought deeply about personal success. It is this: If you want to have any real chance of success in your career, you have to *find the work you love*. That is a contemporary way of saying that you need to discover your vocation in life.

Think of it as what philosophers call a *necessary condition*: it won't guarantee you becoming a success, but you can't be one without it. That is in contrast to what they call a *sufficient condition*, that which does lead directly to success.

The world's business is done by countless people in a great variety of different roles: judges, doctors, plumbers, architects, waiters and so on. Your first task is to find the role that is right for you and then – in the language of the theatre – to 'audition' for it. It may take you several years to identify the right part for yourself in life's drama, but don't give up!

You should be on the lookout to find the highest thing you are capable of doing. This will be determined by the interrelation of your abilities with your environment. Once you have found that highest thing, equip yourself for it and then *do* it. What could be more simple than that?

 Have I found my niche in life, the work I love to do?

Idea 2: Don't settle

Just don't give up trying to do what you really want to do.
Where there is love and inspiration, I don't think you can go
wrong.

Ella Fitzgerald

'Love and inspiration' – if you do find them in your work – are power-ful antidotes against what Shakespeare called 'the slings and arrows of outrageous fortune'. Moreover, they are the two keys that unlock the gate that leads to personal excellence in your working life.

You may at present be finding it difficult to discover your vocation, the work you love to do. But don't throw in the towel too soon. Life is long and it's a quest that often takes time. Don't settle for anything less than the best road for you.

'If it's any consolation', writes bestselling author Wilbur Smith, 'I wandered around like a lost soul for ten years before getting myself on track.' Discouraged by his father from becoming a journalist, Smith qualified as an accountant in his native Northern Rhodesia, now Zambia, before trying his hand at writing. 'Don't despair', he contin-ues, 'there's a role out there for everyone. It just sometimes takes an awful lot of searching for.'

Vocations which we wanted to pursue but did not, bleed like
colours in the whole of our experience.

Honoré de Balzac

Am I wasting my time and energy on pursuits for which I am not fitted?

Idea 3: Three useful indicators

No two of us are born exactly alike. We have different aptitudes which fit us for different jobs.

Plato, *The Republic*

There are three useful practical questions to ask yourself in order to ensure that you are moving in the right direction. They are easy to ask, but you may find that learning the true answers may take you several years. It is not easy to be truthful or realistic about oneself and you need to work with the grain of your nature, not against it.

1 What are your interests?

An interest is a state of feeling in which you wish to pay particular attention to something. Long-standing interests – those activities or pursuits that you naturally like – make it much easier to acquire knowledge and skills in certain fields rather than others.

2 What are your aptitudes?

Aptitudes are your natural abilities, what you are fitted for by disposition. An aptitude is a capacity that may range from being a rare gift or a marked talent to simply being a strength that is slightly above the average or normal.

3 What are the relevant factors in your temperament?

Temperament is an important factor. Some people, for example, need to work outdoors; others prefer an office environment. Some love travel; others do not.

Exercise

Make a list of the following:

My three strongest work-related *interests*:

1

2

3

My three most commented-on *aptitudes*:

1

2

3

Three elements in my *temperament* that influence my career choice:

1

2

3

Idea 4: How to find the right road

Skills vary with the man. We must tread a straight path and strive by that which is born in us.

Pindar, *Odes*, Nemea, 1

Finding that 'straight path' that Pindar talks about can be a challenge, but it is very rarely completely impossible. It's worth the time and effort, although you do have to work at it. As the proverb says,

God gives every bird a worm, but He does not throw it in the nest.

As you acquire a fuller working knowledge of yourself – we never know ourselves completely – it does get a lot easier. You soon know without thinking what would *not* be the right occupation for you, given your unique set – as unique as your DNA – of aptitudes, interests and traits.

Correspondingly, the positive options or feasible career choices open to you seem to reduce themselves in number of their own accord. Therefore they become that much easier to explore. May be after one or two accidental false starts, it dawns on you – suddenly or gradually – that there is really only one road that is open to you. And if you have found the right road you don't need to look for another.

It may seem a very broad or ill-defined road at the time: teaching, for example, but what form of teaching? But you will have moved from what mathematicians call trial-and-error problem solving into the trial-and-improve category, a definite advance.

To know that you are at last in the right field for you does make an enormous difference, as Ralph Waldo Emerson explains:

> *Each man has his own vocation. The talent is the call. There is one direction in which all space is open to him. He has faculties silently inviting him thither to endless exertion. He is like a ship in a river: he runs against obstructions on every side but one; on that side all obstruction is taken away, and he sweeps serenely over a deepening channel into an infinite sea.*

 Have I chosen the right occupation or profession, the one where I can make my optimum contribution for the good of others?

Idea 5: Capability

There is unmapped territory in all of us.

Swedish proverb

We are not in fact bundles of fixed assets – interests, aptitudes, personality – independent of our environment. We are not round pegs looking for round holes. The reality is very different.

There is, in fact, a dynamic relationship between a person and their environment. Einstein gives us a simple definition of the latter:

The environment is everything that isn't me.

The equation between your *talent* – all that you have to offer – and this changing *environment* is what the Victorian writer Thomas Carlyle was the first to call your *capability*:

To each of us is given a certain inward talent, *a certain outward* environment of fortune; *to each, by wisest combination of the two, a certain* maximum *of* capability.

But the hardest problem were ever this first: to find by study of yourself and of the ground you stand on what your combined inward and outward capability *is.*

For, also, our young soul is all budding with capabilities, and we see not yet which is the main and true one...

We live in an age of unprecedented change in our environment. That change decimates some old vocations or occupations. Once, for example, I remember meeting the last 15 of Britain's lighthouse-keepers on a resettlement course. Yet it also creates new ones. My own profession, for instance, did not exist when I was a boy. Nor did today's immense field of information technology – the whole electronic world of the computer and internet in which we live today.

Future changes in the environment may already be creating new opportunities for you, new uses for your existing talent. They may also discover in you new talent, things you have had all along without knowing it. For some of our strengths are dormant or latent until a new challenge brings them to life.

> *'When patterns are broken, new worlds appear.'*

Stay flexible, with one eye always on the changing environment. Be quick to change your skills when the wind shifts or to alter your course when you see a new land appearing on the horizon.

Idea 6: True success

For the cause that lacks assistance,
For the wrong that needs resistance,
For the future in the distance,
And the good that I can do.

George Linnaeus Banks

To succeed, according to the dictionary, means to attain or to be attaining a desired end. Both people and things succeed when they are effective in gaining their purposes or ends, either in particular or in general. The antithesis of success is failure.

What does success mean to you?

Exercise
My object in living is:

People who are commonly described as successful by others are usually doing relatively well financially, it is true. But to be successful implies more than even a modest degree of prosperity: it suggests the fulfillment of certain goals or ambitions, independent of wealth.

What is your desired end? The received wisdom is that the natural desired end – directly or indirectly – is to do the most good we can for others. For we are born to do good. A person is a moral being.

Our means for achieving that end is to use wisely the talent that is ours, and ours alone.

You may have noticed that people who become exceedingly rich as a by-product of being successful in their field, such as Bill Gates, Warren Buffett and Richard Branson, tend to give the greater part of their fortunes away for charitable purposes, to do good in the world. That windfall obligation, incidentally, is part of personal success – that is, success as a person.

You may ask why they do this. The answer is a surprising one – pure pleasure. For, as the Chinese proverb says,

> *The pleasure of doing good is the only one that will not wear out.*

 Do I have a sense of purpose, a clear direction in life?

Idea 7: Success is a result, not a goal

Success usually comes to those who are too busy looking for it.

Henry David Thoreau

When writing down your desired end or purpose in Idea 6 you may have been tempted to keep it simple and put down 'personal success'. After all, it is because you are interested in personal success – for yourself or your children – that I imagine you are reading this book.

Really successful people tell us, however, that success as the world conceives it was never their aim. Indeed, focusing attention on success can, they tell us, be counter-productive. Tennessee Williams wrote:

> *Success is blocked by concentrating on it and planning for it.*
> *Success is shy – it won't come while you are watching.*

If you think of success as a result not a goal, you will also see that luck plays a large part in whether or not it happens to come your way.

So don't let your attention be deflected by the mirage of success, still less its fruits. If it happens, it happens; if not, so what? Not everyone in this uncertain world receives their just deserts. Why should you be an exception? Keep your eye on the true goal.

> *I am never weary of being useful. In serving others I cannot do enough – no labour is sufficient to tire me.*

Leonardo da Vinci

Idea 8: Commitment

I don't know who – or what – put the question,
I don't know when it was put, I don't even remember answering.
But at some moment I did answer Yes to Someone or Something.
And from that hour I was certain that existence is meaningful
And that, therefore, my life, in self-surrender, has a goal.

In this passage from his personal journal *Markings* (1964), Dag Hammarskjöld – the great Secretary General of the United Nations – writes about his own commitment, when almost unaware he discovered that he had become what Wordsworth called 'a dedicated spirit'.

The difference that commitment makes, both in personal as well as professional life, is well captured by W H Murray in his book *Mount Everest Expedition* (1951):

Until one is committed there is hesitancy, the chance to draw back, always ineffectiveness. Concerning all acts of initiative (and creation), there is one elementary truth, the ignorance of which kills countless ideas and splendid plans: that the moment one definitely commits oneself, then Providence moves too.

All sorts of things occur to help one that would never otherwise have occurred. A whole stream of events issues from the decision, raising in one's favour all manner of unforeseen incidents and meetings and material assistance which no man could have dreamt would have come his way.

'Leap and the net will appear.'

Commitment is a choice, for we all have free will. You don't have to commit yourself to anything if you don't want to. But if you do say yes to that elusive someone or something, it does make all the difference. Silently things begin to work; threads appear that will one day join up to form a pattern. As the Italian proverb says,

For a web begun, God sends thread.

Idea 9: Setting aims and objectives

The secret of life is to have a task, something you devote your entire life to, something you bring everything to, every minute of the day for the rest of your life. And the most important thing is, it must be something you cannot possibly complete.

Henry Moore, sculptor

A sculptor like Henry Moore lived with a demanding task-like purpose for his whole life, but he broke it down into a host of small, finite tasks – his sculptures. What is the equivalent process in your field?

We all need an equivalent ability to break down the general into the particular. Purpose and aims have to be solidified into tangible tasks: goals, objectives and targets that can be planned, executed, delivered, and measured or otherwise evaluated.

'If you are going to eat an elephant you need to do it one mouthful at a time.'

Idea 10: Jacob's ladder

Jacob's ladder is a model or framework that gives you a way of connecting up the general to the particular and vice versa.

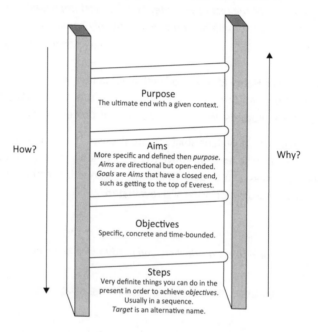

How? ← → Why?

Purpose
The ultimate end with a given context.

Aims
More specific and defined then *purpose*.
Aims are directional but open-ended.
Goals are *Aims* that have a closed end,
such as getting to the top of Everest.

Objectives
Specific, concrete and time-bounded.

Steps
Very definite things you can do in the
present in order to achieve *objectives*.
Usually in a sequence.
Target is an alternative name.

The model or framework is like that fabulous ladder in Jacob's dream in Genesis (28:12): stretching from heaven to earth, with angels descending and ascending.

You can now see that by descending Jacob's ladder, from the general and abstract to the particular and concrete, you are answering the question 'How?' This is my *purpose*. Yes, but *how* are you going to achieve it? By tackling these *aims* or *goals*.

Notice that *aims*, as defined above, are really no more than *purpose* broken down into manageable parts. It is like light being refracted into the colours of the rainbow.

The same is true of the next stage in the descent. Take any one *aim*. How are you going to achieve it? Answer: by achieving these *objectives*.

Now pick out any of these *objectives*: how are you going to accomplish that? Answer: by taking these *steps*. Today? Yes, there's bound to be one of those *steps* that you can take right now!

Going upward on the ladder rather than downward, you are now answering the '*why?*' question. Why are you taking this step? In order to achieve this objective. Why have you set yourself this objective? In order to achieve this particular aim. Why this set of aims? In order to fulfill my purpose.

> '*Nothing is particularly hard if you divide it into small jobs.*'

Idea 11: A forward-looking attitude

A man of hope and forward-looking mind
Even to the last!

William Wordsworth, 'The Excursion'

There are in fact two basic ways of answering the question *why* in the context of the work you do – one backward looking and one forward looking.

The former is modeled on the cause-and-effect relationship.

Q: '*Why* are you doing what you are doing (*effect*)?'
A: 'Because (*cause*) that is how I was told to do it when I joined the profession ten years ago.'

Such a person is like a passenger on a train traveling with his back to the engine and looking out of the window as the past flashes away behind him.

The alternative way of answering the *why* question is signalled by the phrase *in order to*.

Q: '*Why* are you tackling this task?'
A: '*In order to* achieve this aim.'

This person is traveling forward in time, in a seat or attitude that is orientated toward the future.

 The business of life is to go forwards.

Samuel Johnson

Idea 12: Opportunity

The secret of success in life is for a man to be ready for his opportunity when it comes.

Benjamin Disraeli

When people who are successful in their field look back on their life in their later years, they can often identify one or two major turning points on their journey. Often these are times when an unexpected opportunity presented itself, which they had the imagination and judgment to recognize. And they found the courage to respond positively to it and to stretch their capability to new levels of achievement.

Such opportunities rarely come along, and they never tarry to take a sleeping person. So you need both patience and alertness, and a quality that John Keats called negative capability:

At once it struck me what quality went to make a man of achievement, and which Shakespeare possessed so enormously – I mean negative capability, that is when a man is capable of being in uncertainties, mysteries, doubts, without any irritable reaching after fact and reason.

'Luck is what happens when opportunity meets preparation.'

Idea 13: Successes and failures

*If you can meet with Triumph and Disaster
And treat those two imposters just the same...*

Rudyard Kipling

Because successful people tend to work hard, they generate a lot more successes and failures than other people. What they have a knack for doing is to turn their failures into contributors to their eventual success. As Soichiro Honda once said:

Success is 99 percent failure.

After 10,000 attempts to develop the electric light bulb, a friend suggested to Thomas Edison that he should accept defeat. He famously replied:

I have not failed, I've just found 10,000 ways that it won't work.

Exercise

Identify two failures in your working life and two failures in your personal life. Now write down the 'success lessons' that you learnt from each failure.

Looking back, can you see the seeds of today's success in yesterday's failure?

'A minute's success,' wrote the poet Robert Browning, 'pays the failure of years.' But successful people do not rest on their laurels, however hard won. For success can breed complacency or – even worse – inertia. Successful people are always looking ahead to the next goal.

Marie Curie was the first person to win two Nobel Prizes in physics and chemistry, and achieved fame as a pioneer in cancer treatment. Writing in 1894 in a letter to a friend, she said:

> *One never notices what has been done; one can only see what remains to be done.*

'We learn little from victory, much from defeat.'

Idea 14: A shortcut to personal success

He was famous, sir, in his profession.

William Shakespeare, *All's Well That Ends Well*

'To become expert in some field, to acquire mastery in some specific activity to a degree not easily shared by anyone else near by – that is what counts,' said Goethe. Here is your shortcut to success.

In every field there are those who emerge as leaders. They are always masters of their art. They may also acquire a reputation as innovators and pioneers. Most of them are well known within their profession or trade, but not to the outside world. Do you want to be one of them?

To be acknowledged by your fellow professionals is especially reward-ing, for by definition they are more discerning than the general public. Their praise is harder to win. They alone know the intractable problems you face, the difficulties you have to overcome, the true nature of the mastery in your art, and an enduring contribution to the field when they see one.

> *'Recognition is the oxygen of the human spirit.'*

Idea 15: Don't expect an easy ride

The journey is the reward.

Chinese proverb

Living with an open-ended task or purpose in life is never going to be easy. Precise outcomes cannot be determined in advance. A high tolerance for ambiguity and willingness to venture into the unknown is needed.

'Did you ever get lost, having no compass?' a lady once asked the famous Kentuckian frontiersman Daniel Boone, who spent many weeks and even months wandering the vast, trackless and unmapped wilderness.

'No,' he replied, 'I can't say as ever I was lost, but *I was once bewildered for three days.*'

Nor will you be every really satisfied. As Thomas Edison said:

> *Show me a thoroughly satisfied man, and I will show you a failure.*

That is why it is wisely said that success is a journey and not a destination. It is the adventure of being you.

> *I'm proof against that word 'failure'. I've seen behind it. The only failure a man ought to fear, is failure in cleaving to the purposes he sees to be best.*
>
> George Eliot

To be the victim of 'divine discontent' does give you great benefits. To your life's end you will remain interested, committed and challenged, ever looking forward and so ever young at heart.

Your goal is always in front of you, never behind. As Gandhi said,

> *Satisfaction lies in the effort, not in the attainment; full effort is victory.*

It is that fullness of effort – that doing your best – that yields the true glory. Then you can, as the proverb says, leave the results to God.

 Does the path lead upward? Yes, all the way.

Seven Greatest Ideas for Getting On with People

Idea 16: Be pleasant

If you cannot smile, do not open your shop today.

Chinese proverb

Ultimately your talent is just *you*. That is why talent includes attitude as well as aptitude. Your attitude to people is important even on the basic level of self-interest. Others have the power to help or to hinder you, therefore an ability to get on with people is a crucial success factor in life.

 Where would I be today without the help of other people?

To describe a person as pleasant suggests that they are naturally appealing in some way or other, usually because of their kindness, cheerfulness and warmth of heart. Remember in particular that a smile is worth a thousand words.

'Honey catches more flies than vinegar.'

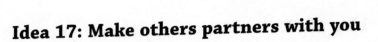

Idea 17: Make others partners with you

I made the soldiers partners with me in the battle.

Field Marshal Lord Montgomery

Some people – not just great leaders – have a way of making you feel as if you are partners with them in some common enterprise. For example, a scientist who worked closely with Einstein once commented that he made you a partner with him in the quest to solve a problem.

The ability to generate that sense of partnership is, I believe, one of the great secrets of success in any field. It happily combines getting on with people with getting things done.

Even more important – and more personally satisfying – you will discover the secret of getting the best out of people. Partnership between people who work together as equals but with complementary skills and responsibilities builds commitment and releases creative energy.

You will find that those whom you perceive and treat as partners will be more generous with their time, knowledge and know-how. Not only from their different skill sets but also from their store of judgment and practical wisdom, they will enrich your business. The path of success is always a shared one.

> *'One head does not contain all the wisdom.'*

Idea 18: Remember to say thank-you

They do not love who do not show their love.

William Shakespeare

If people thank you for what you have done it seems natural; if they don't something is missing.

The reason we feel this way is because our common human nature is deeply reciprocal. Reciprocity is an equal return or counteraction by each of two sides. If you respect people, they will tend to respect you. It is about equivalence in value, but not necessarily in kind.

> *'Unspoken gratitude is useless.'*

The return you make in words should reflect the nature of what has been given or shared with you.

> *The spirit in which a thing is given determines that in which the debt is acknowledged. It's the intention, not the face value of the gift, that's weighted.*
>
> Seneca, *Letters to Lucilius*

Bear that in mind when you thank people for their help.

Idea 19: Use yourself as a gauge

*No man really knows about other human beings. The best he
can do is to suppose that they are like himself.*

John Steinbeck

As Steinbeck says, we don't really know other people, but if you act
on the assumption that they are basically like you it usually works.

The reason is that we are persons, not just individuals. In a person
there is what Coleridge called 'the all in each of every man'. Therefore
we can use ourselves as a gauge in our relations with others. What
works – and does not work – for you or me tells us fairly reliably what
works for others.

The principle is an easy one to remember, if at times a difficult one
to apply.

Do I always use knowledge of myself in shaping my behaviour toward other people?

Idea 20: Share what you know

If wisdom were offered me with the proviso that I should keep it shut up and refrain from declaring it, I should refuse. There's no delight in owning anything unshared.

Seneca, *Letters to Lucilius*

Share what you know with others in your field, and share it generously. The law of reciprocity that I mentioned in Idea 18 will indeed work for you over time in this area as in all others: the more you give the more you will receive. But it will work for you only indirectly over quite long periods of time and often in unexpected ways.

If you do share what you know you will find yourself in an informal network. The best networks are like friendships. They link together those who share a common passion, those who exchange ideas and information in an atmosphere of mutual trust.

> *'It is better to give than receive, but sharing trumps them both.'*

Idea 21: Be trustworthy in word

I do not see how a man can be truly successful who is untrust-worthy in word. When a pin is missing in the yoke-bar of a large cart, how can the cart be expected to go?

Confucius, *Analects* 2:22

Confucius put being trustworthy in word at the top of his list of the qualities that make a successful person. Your word and your action should always march in step together.

This is a simple rule, but an extraordinarily demanding one. It must be, because so few people live up to it.

Exercise
Can you think of three examples in the last month of people who said they would do something and failed to do it?

When was the last time you promised someone that you would do something for them and then failed to follow through with the appropriate action?

'In antiquity', Confucius continued, 'men were loath to speak because they counted it shameful if their person failed to keep up with their words.'

He commended, for example, one ruler named Tzu-lu who 'never put off the fulfillment of a promise to the next day. Better to be halting or make in speech but quick in action!'

As people will ultimately judge you by your actions and not your words, this is sound advice. Waste no time in putting your words into action and then you will build a reputation for being trustworthy.

> 'When you break your word, you break something that cannot be mended.'

Idea 22: Show that you trust people

Evidence of trust begets trust, and love is reciprocated by love.

Plutarch, *Moralia*

There are two basic alternative attitudes to people. You can keep from giving your trust until the other person has proved themselves worthy of it. Or you can trust people until they give you clear signs that they are not to be trusted.

The second strategy is the wiser one of the two. For trust tends to bring out the best in people, and – in some demanding situations – even the greatness that lies within us all.

Trusting others in this way is sometimes thought to be naïve, but that is not the case. This attitude is grounded on thought and conviction, and it doesn't require the surrender of your common sense.

Is a man not superior who, without anticipating attempts at deception or presuming acts of bad faith, is, nevertheless, the first to be aware of such behaviour?

Confucius

'It is better to be sometimes cheated than not to trust.'

Eight Greatest Ideas for Success Qualities

Idea 23: Enthusiasm

I cannot think of any truly successful person who lacks enthusiasm. Can you? This is why it is top of my generic qualities list.

For the Greeks, enthusiasm was a divine gift. The Greek word literally means to be possessed by a god – what we would now call to be inspired. The symptoms of an enthusiastic person are well known: a lively or strong interest for a cause or activity; a great eagerness; an intense and sometimes even passionate zeal for the work in hand.

You can see why Shakespeare in *Henry IV* identifies enthusiasm as 'the very lifeblood of our enterprise'. It is the lifeblood of your enterprise too.

Nowadays passion is often used as a synonym for enthusiasm. Passion is actually a much stronger word, suggesting something that stirs deep within and is sometimes ungovernable. Enthusiasm, by contrast, is broader in scope. It encompasses, for example, a lively or eager interest in something or someone or a glowing admiration for a cause or activity, or for a wide mixture of all of these things.

> *Nothing great in this world was achieved without enthusiasm.*
>
> Ralph Waldo Emerson

The importance of enthusiasm is that it is a sustainable rocket fuel for all effective work. It compels action. It sends you into your natural orbit and sustains you effortlessly there. It is actually difficult to be very effective without this enthusiasm for what you are doing. Certainly, without it, excellence in performance will elude you.

It is the calling of a teacher, parent and leader to locate and ignite this fuel of enthusiasm. My favourite definition of a true teacher is 'one whose actual lesson may be forgotten, but whose living enthusiasm is a quickening, animating and inspiring power'.

Enthusiasm is linked also to energy or vitality and also to creativeness. People with a real zest for their work – dynamic vigour along with uninhibited enjoyment – often have the kind of physical and mental energy that keeps them going when others are flagging or when they have had little sleep.

Can I go from failure to failure without losing my enthusiasm?

Idea 24: Tenacity

Let me tell you the secret that hassled me to my goal. My strength lies solely in my tenacity.

Louis Pasteur

In her great book *Function, Purpose and Powers* (1958), the British philosopher Professor Dorothy Emmet wrote:

If vocational people work from some inner incentive proper to themselves, they will tend to be, or rather perhaps to become, strong characters. They will need to develop considerable powers of concentration, and the ability to go on in spite of discouragements. In so far as their work can also be looked on as role behaviour (and from the point of view of one kind of social analysis all work is this), they will be likely to perform their roles in ways individual to themselves...

How original a person dares to be in carrying out a role may largely depend on how strong a character he or she is.

Tenacity means holding firmly on to your purpose. Persistence, perseverance, unwillingness to admit defeat, stubbornness in adversity – all these are variations on the same theme. Sticking to your aim, however, doesn't imply that kind of mindless consistency that Emerson once called 'the hobgoblin of little minds'. You can be tenacious about ends while being completely flexible about means.

There are but two roads that lead to an important goal and to the doing of great things – strength and perseverance. Strength is the lot of a few privileged men; but austere perseverance, steady and continuous, may be employed by the smallest of us and rarely fails of its purpose, for its silent power grows irresistibly greater with time.

Johann Wolfgang von Goethe, German writer

There must be a beginning in any great matter, but the continuing unto the end until it be thoroughly finished yields the true glory.

Sir Francis Drake, Elizabethan sailor and navigator

Idea 25: Hard work

The dictionary is the only place where success comes before work.

Mark Twain

Hard refers to tasks for mind or body and means demanding great toil and effort in reaching the appointed or desired end – it is diametrically opposed to all that is *easy*.

Perhaps the most evident common denominator of truly successful people is that they show that kind of sustained diligence. 'I was made to work', said Johann Sebastian Bach, and added: 'If you are equally industrious, you will be equally successful.' Well...

What is certainly true is that footprints in the sands of time are not made by sitting down. Most real achievement in any field calls for great effort. The saying attributed to Thomas Edison, that genius is 10 percent inspiration and 90 percent perspiration, holds true for us lesser mortals.

Incidentally, talking about Edison, he once commented:

> *One may think that the money value of an invention constitutes its reward to the man who loves his work. But speaking for myself, I can honestly say this is not so... I continue to find my greatest pleasure – and so my reward – in the work that precedes what the world calls success.*

Diligence derives from the Latin verb 'to love, to take pleasure in'. The good news is that for those who have found the work they love to do it doesn't *seem* like hard work, at least not like the 'hard labour' that may be a consequence of going to prison. As the entertainer and playwright Noël Coward, author of an autobiography entitled *A Talent to Amuse*, once said:

Fun is not as much fun as work.

In fact, to become a master in any profession takes not only natural aptitude but long study and constant practice. Yes, it's strenuous, often arduous and usually difficult work – but who wants cheap success?

 You cannot plough a field by turning it over in your mind.

The famous violinist Fritz Kreisler was once stopped outside the concert hall by an enthusiastic member of the audience.

'I would give my life to play the violin the way you do,' the man said.

'I did,' replied Kreisler.

Idea 26: Generosity of spirit

He gives nothing who does not give himself.

French proverb

Generosity of spirit means that in all the transactions and relationships of life, you are oriented to give more than you receive – indeed, sometimes to give without any thought of receiving. The law of reciprocity is such, however, that *the more you give, the more you receive.*

Henry Ford expressed the same principle in a commercial context:

> *A man who will use his skill and constructive imagination to see how much he can give for a dollar, instead of how little he can give for a dollar, is bound to succeed.*

Generosity of spirit is revealed in a willingness to go the extra mile, to serve others beyond the letter of the contract and to do what needs to be done – not the minimum that one is paid to do. That is the key to creating a delighted customer.

Painting frescoes in the Sistine Chapel, Michelangelo was lying on his back on a high scaffold, carefully outlining a figure in a corner of the ceiling. A friend asked him why he took such pains with such an obscure figure, one that would be many feet above the head of the viewer in the ill-lit chapel.

'After all,' added the friend, 'who will know whether it is perfect or not?'

'I will,' said Michelangelo.

Try not to become a man of success, but rather a man of value. He is considered successful in our day who gets more out of life than he puts in. But a man of value will give more than he receives.

Albert Einstein

Idea 27: Imagination

In dreams begin our possibilities.

William Shakespeare

Did Shakespeare set himself the strategic goal of becoming the world's most famous playwright and then plan his plays accordingly? It is highly improbable that he thought that way. But he may have dreamed of greatness when he was a boy. As the Spanish proverb says:

> *If you build no castles in the air, you build no castles anywhere.*

Successful people tend to be imaginative on different levels. In decision-making or problem-solving situations, for example, imagination is the ability and drive to discern the various useful possibilities and alternatives that are inherent in a problem, but are not obvious to less perceptive observers.

Imagination – the art of seeing things that are invisible –goes hand in hand with creativity. Walt Disney once said:

> *If you can* dream *it, you can* do *it.*

So often it is your imagination that lights the slow fuse to your greatest achievements.

Idea 28: Courage

Courage is the father of success.

Nigerian proverb

Our fears are usually about the future. Most of the things we fear never happen, and most of the rest don't turn out the way we expect them to happen. Nonetheless, fears are real and you can't make them disappear. With practice, however, you can recognize them for what they are and do your best to override them. For courage doesn't mean being unafraid but not allowing oneself to be invaded and held hostage by fear.

> *If you have a dangerous job to do, you can't really let the thought of the danger enter your mind. Once it's in your mind it's very difficult to cast it out. So somehow you've got to guard your mind. Some find it easier to do than others. Undoubtedly one thing that helps is concentration on your job.*

Group Captain Leonard Cheshire VC

Once people are caught up in an event and become busy, it is true that they often cease to be afraid. Your mind cannot focus on two things at once.

In one's vocational life there are probably only one, two or three big decisions – decisions that call not only for good judgment but also for courage. As Shakespeare wrote:

> *There is a tide in the affairs of men,*
> *Which, taken at the flood, leads on to fortune;*
> *Omitted, all the voyage of their life*
> *Is bound in shallows and in miseries...*
> *And we must take the current when it serves,*
> *Or lose our ventures.*

At what point in my career or personal life have I made a decision that called for courage?

Idea 29: Integrity

Trust being lost, all the social intercourse of men is brought to nothing.

Livy, Roman historian

Success in any business or field depends on building good personal relationships with other people, especially those who are there to help you. And the bedrock or foundation of *all* personal relationships – business or private – is integrity.

Field Marshal Lord Slim once defined integrity to me as 'the quality which makes people trust you'. Mutual trust between the leader and the led is absolutely vital: lose that and you have lost everything. Moreover, it is very hard to re-establish it.

Integrity, from the Latin *integer*, literally means wholeness: an integer is a whole number. But with reference to people, it signifies the trait that comes from a loyal adherence to values or standards *outside yourself*, especially the truth. It is a wholeness which stems from being true to truth.

We know what it means when people say of a scholar or artist that he or she has integrity. They do not deceive themselves or other people. They are not manipulators. As Oliver Cromwell once wrote in a letter to a friend:

Subtlety may deceive you, integrity never will.

Just why it is that people who have integrity in this sense create trust in others I shall leave you to reflect on at your leisure. Certainly we all know that a person who deliberately misleads us by telling lies sooner or later forfeits our trust.

There are situations in life that can test your integrity, sometimes to the uttermost. A person of integrity is able to come through such trials, tests and temptations.

 Do I agree that integrity – the quality that makes people trust you – is the necessary condition for all good and long-lasting relationships, business or personal?

Idea 30: Humility

The arrogant man has no friends.

Moroccan proverb

Humility is not being arrogant. Humility is simply knowing the truth about yourself, so it is the enemy of self-abasement as well as self-exultation.

Willingness to own up to your own mistakes or errors of judgment rather than to make others into scapegoats is one hallmark of humility. Domineering, over-assertive or tyrannical men or women don't do that – they are always right even when their ship is sinking.

Another important characteristic is open-mindedness to those views and opinions of others that challenge your own ideas or assumptions. Humble people make good listeners.

Humility also means that you know what you don't know, and so you remain throughout your life open to learning, ready to change and willing to grow.

'Real excellence and humility walk hand in hand.'

Follow-up test

Finding the work you love

☐ If you are on the right road you do not need to look for another. Have you found yet your right role in your working life yet? If not, do you remain determined to find work that you can do whole-heartedly?

☐ Did aptitudes, interests and temperament play a part in your eventual choice of career, and if so in what ways?

☐ Has the changing environment altered your ideas about your personal capability?

☐ Do you have a working definition, one that reflects your values, of your purpose and chief aims for working?

☐ Is personal success for you the all-consuming goal, or do you see it as a desirable result of employing your talent to the full?

☐ Can you list the three great commitments in your life?

☐ Are you skilled in relating closed objectives to open aims?

☐ Is your focus on the future rather than the past?

☐ Would you describe yourself as prepared or ready for the kind of opportunity you are seeking?

☐ Do you have a positive but realistic attitude to both your successes and your failures?

☐ Make a list of the five success criteria that you would now use for assessing whether or not – or how far – another person's life is a success story. How high have you placed reputation within your trade, craft, art or profession?

☐ If success is a journey and not a destination, are you prepared for it not to be an easy one?

Getting on with people

☐ Are there any changeable aspects in your personality that make you difficult to get on with? If so, do you have a strategy for dealing with them?

☐ Do you generate a sense of partnership with those who work with you?

☐ Do you never miss an opportunity to say a sincere 'thank-you'?

☐ Have you found yourself – what works for you – to be a reliable gauge for what you say or do to others?

☐ By sharing your knowledge with others in your field, have you built up a network, 'a community of purpose'?

☐ Are your words and actions in perfect harmony?

☐ 'Trust people and they will be trustworthy, treat them as great and they will show you their greatness.' How far do these words reflect your own attitude?

Success qualities

☐ Can you think of three people in the last six months who have commented – directly or indirectly – on your enthusiasm?

☐ Are you still pursuing your purpose with tenacity, despite the setbacks and disappointments that you have experienced along the way?

☐ Do you put in the hours?

☐ If you don't have much imagination yourself, do you value it in others and harvest the fruits of their ideas?

☐ Can you think of one crisis in your career when you needed to act with courage?

☐ 'Integrity – adherence to the truth outside yourself – is the quality that makes people trust you.' Do you agree?

☐ Do you strive to eliminate any trace of arrogance in the way you relate to both your work and to other people?

'Every calling is great when greatly pursued.'

PART TWO

Using Your Time to Good Effect

Let every man be master of his time.
William Shakespeare, *Macbeth*, III. i. 48

If you wish to achieve personal success in your profession or field, you do need to become a master at managing your time. For time is your scarcest and most precious resource. In a sense, it is your life.

There are two simple aspects to being a good time manager. First, you need to ensure that your time is going on the right things. Is it 'turning wheels and making things happen'? Secondly, you should avoid wasting time. As you know, there are plenty of ways in which that can happen.

Equally importantly, you should respect the time of other people. People may work for you or with you, but that doesn't give you a licence to waste their time.

No one learns to be a master of their time in a day. If you reflect on how you are actually spending your time, at any point in your life you will find that there is always room for improvement.

Six Greatest Ideas for Developing a Personal Sense of Time

Idea 31: Time used well is life

Time wasted is existence, used is life.

Edward Young, English poet

'Remember that time is money,' wrote US Founding Father Benjamin Franklin in *Advice to a Young Tradesman* (1748). In 1723 Franklin had run away from his Puritan parents in New England, but not before he had imbibed the Puritan virtues of thrift, industry and conscientiousness.

'Do you love life?' said Franklin. 'Then do not squander time, for that is the stuff life is made of.'

Both time and money are limited resources. That is the point of the analogy. Therefore time (like money) is a valuable commodity. It can be borrowed, saved or squandered – all words springing from the original and basic analogy. Indeed, there is a whole system of smaller metaphors under the 'time is money' umbrella, such as:

> *Yesterday is a cancelled check.*
> *Tomorrow is a promissory note.*
> *Today is ready cash. Use it!*

All analogies break down at a certain point. Time is patently *not* money. It is only when we begin to think about the ways in which it is not money that our sense of its uniqueness comes home. You can make money; you can't make time. Money isn't finite. Sand in the hourglass isn't like money in the bank. As the Chinese proverb says:

> *A yard of gold cannot buy an inch of time.*

Time really is infinitely *more* precious than money.

The 'time is money' analogy is operational, not a mere literary orna-
ment. It is a positive and practical help to look on time as money. For
money is a widespread yardstick of value. If we see our time as being
more valuable than money we have it about right. As most of us try
to save our money and invest it wisely, how much more should we
try to avoid wasting our time and to invest it with energy to good
effect?

> *You have to live on this twenty-four hours of daily time. Out of*
> *it you have to spin health, pleasure, money, content, respect,*
> *and the evolution of your immortal soul. Its right use, its most*
> *effective use, is a matter of the highest urgency and of the most*
> *thrilling actuality. All depends on that.*
>
> Arnold Bennett, *How to Live on Twenty-Four Hours* (1907)

Idea 32: Setting your course

It's not enough to be busy. The question is: What are you busy about?

Henry Thoreau

The first and greatest Principle of War – 'Selection and Maintenance of the Aim' – also applies to peace. As John Milton wrote,

Peace has its victories.

Your purpose or chief aim is more like the Pole Star – you won't ever reach it or touch it, but it does give you a sense of direction in life. It divides mere busy-ness from purposeful busy-ness. Avoid Alice's condition in Lewis Carroll's fable:

'Cheshire Puss ... would you tell me, please, which way I ought to go from here?'

'That depends a good deal on where you want to get to,' said the Cat.

'I don't much care where–' said Alice.

'Then it doesn't matter which way you go,' said the Cat.

'– so long as I get somewhere,' Alice added as an explanation.

'Oh, you're sure to do that,' said the Cat, 'if you only walk long enough.'

Even if you are working hard but on the wrong agenda, you are still wasting your time and thus your life.

Am I now clear about my chief aim?
Do I know what I want to do to effect it?
Do I know what lies outside my focus?

Idea 33: A sense of purpose

From the gods comes the saying 'Know thyself'.

Juvenal, *Satires*, 2nd century BCE

Your energy and your personal effectiveness flow from your sense of purpose. Understanding and developing that sense of purpose are not intuitive. They are usually a product of introspection and being aware of your situation, and integrating all these things together.

You should distinguish between *action thinking* – identifying objectives, making plans, evaluating or reviewing results – and *reflective thinking*. Here you are standing back and taking a helicopter view of your life: who you are, where you have come from, where you are going. More specifically, you will be thinking about yourself in relation to your role, and your role in relation to a changing and challenging environment.

Looking back on the last three months, have I invested any time in reflective thinking?

We tend to think of truly successful people as being very extrovert and action centred. But there is research to show that excellent leaders – as opposed to very good leaders – are distinctly more reflective than their counterparts.

It's no good trying to shine if you don't take time to fill your lamp.

Robert Browning

Idea 34: Sell to yourself on benefits

Go, sir, gallop, and don't forget that the world was made in six days. You can ask me for anything you like, except time.

Napoleon

The first law of salesmanship is that you sell benefits, not products or services as such. And that is true if you are trying to sell an idea to yourself, especially one that is going to call for sustained effort, the painstaking construction of daily habits and a commitment to continuous incremental improvement.

The benefits of not wasting your time in doing the wrong things, or merely frittering it away on trivialities, are:

◆ *Time to think* – Time for both action thinking and also reflective thinking.
◆ *Time for your people* – If you have saved time you can give it, your most precious resource, with a generous spirit to those who need to talk to you.
◆ *Time for customers* – We all have customers of one kind or another. Business is about building relationships, and that takes time – your time.

Exercise
Assuming that you did make time to think – either action thinking or reflective thinking – in the next week, what would be the three most important items on your agenda?

Idea 35: Making time to think

One of the most impressive leaders I have known personally was Field Marshal Lord Montgomery. He believed that any leader in a high position must be ruthless about one thing – the use of his time. Listen to what he has to say:

> What advice can be offered to a leader: He must discipline himself and lead a carefully regulated and ordered life. He must allow a certain amount of time for quiet thought and reflection; the best times are in the early morning, and in the evening. The quality, good or bad, of any action which is to be taken will vary directly with the time spent in thinking; against this, he must not be rigid; his decisions and plans must be readily adaptable to changing situations. A certain ruthlessness is essential, particularly with inefficiency and also with those who would waste his time. People will accept this, provided the leader is ruthless with himself ...
>
> Most leaders will find there is so much to do and so little time to do it; that was my experience in the military sphere. My answer to that is not to worry; what is needed is a quiet contemplation of all aspects of the problem, followed by a decision – and it is fatal to worry afterwards.

Idea 36: A sense of perspective

All the troubles of life come upon us because we refuse to sit quietly for a while each day in our rooms.

Blaise Pascal,
French philosopher and mathematician

For some people a time of quiet and reflection is a daily necessity. As Peter Walker, a former British Secretary of State, points out, one of the benefits of reflective thinking is a sense of perspective:

At some stage during the day, often during the evening, I make time for an hour's meditation. I sit in an armchair, perhaps with a glass of whisky, and consider what's going to happen tomorrow. I think of what the importance of it all is. I think of family things.

What it does is to put life into perspective. Something which at 10am seemed a terrible worry is no longer a worry when viewed in the context of what life is all about. I think that's why I'm a placid person. For some people a small event can become an obsession. Meditation stops one being constantly impetuous and in politics that's important. Leo Amery first advised me to meditate and now having done it for 16 or 17 years I couldn't do without it.

I never worry about what the future holds in politics. I take things as they come, otherwise there's too much to worry about. First you worry about becoming an MP; then you worry about becoming a minister of state, chancellor, foreign secretary or prime minister. And when you reach any of those positions you worry about losing them. If you are crazy enough to do that you will not enjoy politics.

Practical meditation of this kind can change your life. Spiritually you need such times of silence and solitude. It's no good trying to shine if you don't take time to fill your lamp.

Try getting away from your office and going to sit in a quiet place, such as the public library. A change of environment helps you to think.

Seven Greatest Ideas for Major Time Savers

Idea 37: Learning to say no

The real discipline comes in saying no to the wrong opportunities.

Peter Drucker

Effectiveness at work depends on knowing what *not* to do. Over-commitment is a sure road to failure.

You may find it hard to refuse someone's request for your time. Possibly you feel that the other person will think less of you for doing so. Learn to decline with tact and firmness.

When you say 'no', if possible say it promptly. Thus you will avoid raising false hopes only for them to be dashed later. Such vague phrases as 'Let me think about it' or 'I don't know' do breed expectancy. Of course, if you are in genuine doubt, by all means play for time. Ask for more information, perhaps in the form of a written request with background data.

Remember that you do have the right to say no. Although it is normally courteous to give a reason, even an invented one, you do not have to excuse yourself every time you turn down a request. Politeness is never out of place. Be sensitive as well; you may think you have more important matters to attend to but the other person may have different ideas. What is important and what is not depends to some extent on where you are sitting.

Know your opportunity cost

If you say yes to one request and commit your time in the future, you have lost your freedom to respond to an opportunity that might arise before you have to deliver. This calls for judgment on your part, for sometimes a bird in the hand is better than three birds on the wing.

The *opportunity cost* is the loss you incur when you're doing one thing instead of another. You have lost the value of the thing you choose not to do. When you take on something new, make sure you understand what you'll have to stop doing to make time for the new task.

 You have to find ways of saying 'no' firmly but politely. If you want to get things done, you have to become good at turning down opportunities that don't fit into your strategy.

Learning to say no is a phrase of four simple words. But as a practice it is your most important time saver.

Idea 38: Delegate, delegate, delegate

The more important your job, the more you need to delegate. The pressures and demands on your time are too great even if you had 48 hours in your day and not 24. Montgomery (Idea 35) was able to have time to think because he delegated all operational business to his corps commanders and all staff or administrative business to his very able chief-of-staff. That is how it should be.

So, what qualities must you have to be a good delegator? There are five main tips:

1   Choose the right staff.
2   Train them.
3   Take care in briefing them, and ensuring their under-standing of the 'why' and 'how to' of tasks delegated to them (and impart to them an understanding of business aims and policies).
4   Try not to interfere – stand back and support.
5   Control in a sensible and sensitive manner by checking progress at agreed intervals.

Checklist for effective delegation

☐ Do you take work home at evenings/weekends and/or work more than nine hours a day?

☐ Can you identify areas of work that you could/should del-egate, but have not already done so?

☐ Do you define clearly the delegated tasks and satisfy your-self that the individual to whom they are delegated under-stands what is expected as an outcome?

☐ Can you trust people, or do you find it difficult to do so?
☐ Do you delegate authority and tasks?
☐ Do you think that the delegated task will not be done as well by anyone else?
☐ Do you involve those to whom tasks have been delegated in the whole planning and problem-solving process?

'You will never have so much authority as when you begin to give it away.'

Idea 39: Always do what you say you will

Have you noticed how much of your time is wasted in chasing up people who said that they will do something for you and then don't do it?

If you always do what you say you will – on time and according to specification – you will not only save your own time but the other person's time as well. They won't have to waste time chasing *you*. Your own personal example will give you the moral authority to expect others to deliver according to the agreed decision. Indeed, if you are a leader you should insist on it, otherwise you cannot make things happen.

'No sooner said than done.'

Idea 40: Avoid procrastinating

Procrastination – putting off until tomorrow (and tomorrow and tomorrow) what you should do today – is the proverbial 'thief of time'. Everyone procrastinates sometimes, but for some people it becomes a bad habit.

Procrastination might be defined as the act of delaying starting or completing tasks that you consider important. It's a form of self-sabotage: you are simply handicapping yourself.

Chronic procrastinators give you reasons, but they are really rationalizations or excuses. One way of avoiding the risk of failure is to do nothing. But, as Shakespeare said, 'nothing will come of nothing', least of all any form of personal success.

> *He slept beneath the moon,*
> *He basked beneath the sun*
> *He lived a life of going-to do*
> *And died with nothing done.*
>
> Epitaph of James Albert (1838–89)

It is usually the unpleasant things that get pushed forward from day to day. If you want to be successful, however, you need the courage not to evade unpleasant situations and the practical wisdom in order to deal most effectively with them.

Idea 41: Don't waste time on the past

Time wastes our bodies and our wits,
But we waste Time, so we are quits.

Writing on a sundial from 1746

The focus of your active thinking time and your reflective thinking time should be on the present and the future, not the past. The reason is that the past is fixed; you cannot decide anything or do anything about it. Crying over spilt milk, as the proverb puts it, is a complete waste of your time.

Failures, mistakes and errors all have lessons for the present and the future. Once you have teased them out and taken them on board, turn your face to the future once more, to 'fresh fields and pastures new'.

The Inn of Memory has some pleasant memories and also some painful ones. Visit the Inn occasionally, but don't let the Innkeeper persuade you to take up residence. In order to pursue the chief aim of your life, you belong on the road that leads forward in time.

So put your energy into the present and the future. Feeling sorry for yourself or torturing yourself over past mistakes is a colossal waste of time. It is far better spent on doing what you need to do now to make things better. While you may not see any immediate results, acting in the present is far better than feeling sorry for yourself about the past.

> *'Mistakes in the past are stepping stones to success.'*

Idea 42: Don't make the same mistake twice

To stumble twice against the same stone is a proverbial disgrace.

Cicero

Many mistakes, such as forgetting your passport or traveling without a valid visa and being refused entry to another country, are both frustrating and time wasting. To repeat such mistakes is indeed 'a proverbial disgrace'.

Lessons learnt the hard way are often both painful and memorable so that we are programmed against repeating them again. As the proverb says:

Once bitten, twice shy.

If you do find yourself repeating mistakes, ask yourself why. The pattern may indicate that there is something that needs changing in your habits, your attitudes or your systems. Correct the underlying cause and you will eliminate this particular time waster from your life.

> *'The best way to run out of mistakes is to never make the same mistake twice.'*

Idea 43: Cut your losses

Because we never – or very seldom – have as much information as we would like, there is always a trial-and-error element to our best endeavours. One of the hardest judgment calls is knowing when to cut your losses.

It is hard to do this, because successful people tend to be tenacious. But they are also realistic. Reinforcing failure, as it is called, is extremely wasteful of all resources, not merely your time.

Intuition usually tells you when to call it a day. Be decisive. The sooner you cut your losses, the quicker you can move on to what you need to be doing. If you don't let go, you worsen the loss.

What also makes it hard to cut your losses is the degree of emotional investment and involvement that you and others have put into the project. You need to be able to transcend that emotion and look objectively at the situation – to see it as it really is and be wary of false hopes or groundless optimism.

It's human nature to shrink in the face of bad news or disappointment, and to hope that something will happen to make the situation better. But something magical usually doesn't happen, and the time we waste in denial is always crucial.

 You need judgment born of experience to know when to cut your losses – not too soon and not too late.

Five Greatest Ideas for Principles of Planning

Idea 44: The skill of planning

The business of life is to go forwards.

Samuel Johnson

Planning is one of the key functions of leadership (see Idea 65), but it's also pretty crucial for leading your life. You can turn a necessary function like planning into a skill by study and practice – lots of practice.

The study part, incidentally, helps you to learn from the experience of others – much more time – and cost-effective! As importantly, it gives you the opportunity to learn the key principles that you need to improve your practice.

In a given calendar period, assuming that you are not starting from scratch, a group of objectives or plans will be at various stages of completion. It is like managing a portfolio of shares, each with its particular contribution and level of performance.

The plan should outline in appropriate detail what steps have to be taken in order to complete the task. When you have thought forward, try thinking backward from the visualized point of task completion to the present. This will help you to avoid leaving out essential steps.

A good plan will always answer the questions: Who? When? Where? How? What? and Why? Whether you're in doubt or otherwise, it is wise to check your plans with someone else. You may be making some unconscious assumptions that another person will swiftly spot. Two heads are better than one.

What an operational plan will *not* do for you is make anything happen. It can be no more than an architect's blueprint. If you are only an architect and not a builder, nothing will happen.

'Fail to plan and you plan to fail.'

If you want to enjoy one of the greatest luxuries in life, the luxury of having enough time, time to rest, time to think things through, time to get things done and know you have done them to the best of your ability, remember there is only one way. Take enough time to think and plan things in order of their importance. Your life will take a new zest, you will add years to your life, and more life to your years. Let all your things have their places. Let each part of your business have its time.

Benjamin Franklin, US Founding Father and politician

Idea 45: The worst-case scenario

What practice in planning and the resultant experience teach is that once you start implementing them, the plans rarely work out the way you predict they will. There are usually surprises – sometimes unpleasant ones. Therefore it is vital to stay flexible, which means being able to modify or change your plans as unforeseen circumstances unfold.

Master planners always like to imagine the *worst-case scenario*. Here is Napoleon at work, in a letter to his brother Joseph:

> *I am used to thinking three or four months in advance about what I must do, and I calculate on the worst. In war nothing is achieved except by calculations. Everything that is not soundly planned in its details yields no results.*

Napoleon was not a man to leave things to chance. Should you?

> 'A plan is a very good basis for changing your mind.'

Idea 46: The planning/implementation ratio

If I had eight hours to chop down a tree I'd spend six sharpening my axe.

Abraham Lincoln

Imagine two groups tackling the same common task. Group A skimps on planning. The leader is action centred in the wrong sense of that phrase – he regards thinking as a waste of time. As a consequence, Group A takes a long time to complete the task. Nobody in that group is clear on the objective; alternative courses of action have not been explored.

By contrast, Group B takes adequate time to plan. The objective is made clear and definite; time limits and other boundaries are clarified. The optimum course of action or solution is chosen from a list of feasible options. There may even have been a brainstorming session to help generate creative ideas. Everyone feels committed. The job gets done faster.

Planning/Implementation Ratio

Group A	
PLANNING	IMPLEMENTATION

Group B	
PLANNING	IMPLEMENTATION

A casual observer in the planning phase may have given marks to the leader of Group A for decisiveness. But looking at the exercise overall it is clear who made the better decisions.

The principle that 'planning saves time' applies to individuals as well as teams or organizations. Always work on this key principle:

Every moment spent planning saves three or four in execution.

Idea 47: Setting objectives

There is a skill in the general leadership function of *defining the task*. In this context, goals or objectives should be definite in the sense of being well defined. Objectives are tangible and near at hand. The archery target is a good analogy here. Goals may imply more distance or greater difficulty.

Like silver, the genuine article should bear certain hallmarks, such as being specific, measurable and subject to a deadline.

Exercise

Tick the boxes for the five most important hallmarks that a well-defined objective should have on this list:

Checklist – Hallmarks of good objectives

☐ Clear	☐ Realistic
☐ Specific	☐ Challenging
☐ Measurable	☐ Agreed
☐ Attainable	☐ Consistent
☐ Written	☐ Worthwhile
☐ Time-bounded	☐ Participative

Idea 48: Time for reflective thinking

Follow effective action with quiet reflection. From the quiet reflection will come more effective action.

Peter Drucker

A plan gives you something to work on, but it is only half the battle. The other half is to implement it. 'Plans are only good *intentions*,' Peter Drucker once told me, 'unless they degenerate into hard work.'

It is unlikely that everything will go according to plan. You may well have on your hands what the British Army calls a 'limited success'. Time for some reflective thinking.

Look in particular at any objectives you failed to achieve in the period under review. What went wrong? There are four possible causes listed in the table. But avoid blaming external circumstances too much: it can become a habit.

Diagnosing causes of limited success

CIRCUMSTANCES BEYOND YOUR CONTROL	Could you not have foreseen these circumstances four or six months ago? What indicators did you ignore?
CIRCUMSTANCES WITHIN YOUR CONTROL	Were there factors within your control, such as recruiting enough staff, which you ignored or handled badly? Did the failure lie within your powers as an implementer rather than planner?
INSUFFICIENT MOTIVATION	Did you write down four or six months ago some objectives that you had no real intention of completing? Goals are demanding: did the difficulty involved reveal your lack of motivation?

INSUFFICIENT SKILL IN SETTING OBJECTIVES	Review the actual goals or objectives against the 12 'Hallmarks of good objectives' in Idea 47. Did the lack of a deadline, for example, explain why the job was not done on time?

People often rationalize failures that are due to their own shortcomings by blaming factors that they assume, claim or pretend were outside their dominion.

You can only learn how to set objectives by setting them and by reviewing your performance afterwards. In the case of limited success, thinking backward after the expiry date should enable you to identify which of the four causes of limited success led to failure. Don't make the same mistake three times!

Six Greatest Ideas for Effective Daily Work

Idea 49: Plan your day

Where no plan is laid, where the disposal of time is surrendered merely to the chance of incidents, chaos will soon reign.

Victor Hugo, French writer

At the end of each day, write down the five things – plus or minus two – that you plan to do tomorrow. This is your familiar to-do list.

In the framework I suggested earlier of Jacob's ladder (Idea 10), these are steps that lead you toward attaining your goals or objectives.

Remember also to remain flexible. Someone – such as a family member or important customer – may put in a claim on your time and they may deserve a higher priority than the next item on your list.

What is the best use of my time right now? That is the question you should be asking yourself continually throughout the day. The answers must be related to constantly changing circumstances and the needs of the minute, yet they must not be mutually self-defeating in the longer term. It is essentially a series of value judgments, requiring from you a rare measure of mental discipline in the service of an unerring sense of time.

Planning your day should not be done in a few minutes on the back of an envelope. Budget a reasonable time for your daily planning. Some people like to do it at the beginning of the day's work. Others prefer to plan their day the night before. This has the advantage that you can sleep on it. Sometimes after a night's rest, other points for your list will occur to you or you may alter your priorities. Your subconscious mind will often suggest these alterations, like a computer doing its work for you.

You have to invest time in order to save time.

Idea 50: Prioritize – no, really prioritize

Keep the general goal in sight while tackling daily tasks.

Chinese proverb

A priority is composed of two elements in various mixtures: *urgency* and *importance*. Repairing that punctured tyre on your car is urgent, but it is not important. It is important that you begin to think about next year's marketing strategy, but it is not urgent. But it is both urgent and important that you convince the chief executive about new sales campaigns at your 4.30 pm meeting today.

Your plan of action for the day should follow these rules:

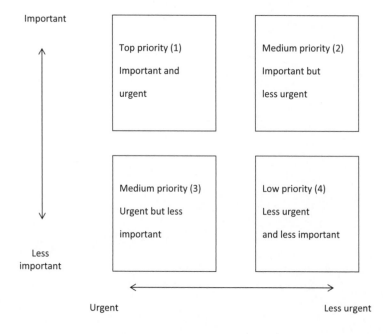

Prioritizing means rating the various tasks that you have an opportunity to carry out. You need good judgment to make good choices about what's important. Nothing and no one is perfect – you just have to give it your best.

Learn to pick out the one or two things that really have to get done – the one or two things that hold 80 percent of the value for your business (see Idea 51 on the Pareto principle). Then make sure that those one or two things get done.

'Be ruthless about priorities: pick one or two things that really need to get done.'

Idea 51: The Pareto principle

The Pareto principle, named after an Italian economist, states that the significant items of a given group form a relatively small part of the total. For example, 20 percent of the sales force will bring in 80 percent of new business. As that ratio seems to hold true in many areas, it is often called the 80:20 rule or the concept of 'the vital few and trivial many'.

Other writers have already applied this principle to time management. It is especially useful in coping with daily lists of action points. Most of the benefits will be related to two or three items. Select these key items and allocate blocks of consolidated time to achieve them.

The Pareto principle also relates to the time available in your day: 80 percent of your really productive and creative work will be done in 20 percent of your time. Not just any old 20 percent. By now you should know clearly which four or five hours of the day constitute your prime time.

Making best use of your best time

Your best time is simply when you do your best work. For most people it is early in the morning, with performance tailing off by lunchtime. Use this time for your most important work. The early bird usually catches the worm.

You will get the most out of your prime hours if you give some study to the laws of creative thinking. Preparation in the form of problem analysis and information collecting is especially valuable. Understanding how your mind works, especially the depth mind principle (see Idea 86), is also a great help. It enables you to work with nature and not against it.

About 20 percent of my time will produce 80 percent of my productive output. Can I afford not to manage at least *that* 20 percent?

Start tomorrow with those four or five hours and it could change your life.

Idea 52: How to control interruptions

Distinguish between interruptions. Some are good; some are tolerable; and some are avoidable. A conscious act of judgment should govern your response. Once you are interrupted, employ some of the damage-control hints listed below.

You should plan in order to minimize the number of unwelcome interruptions if you're going to manage effectively. One hour of concentrated work is worth four hours broken into five-minute fragments by unwanted callers or trivial telephone queries; to reimmerse yourself in a report after each interruption takes time. So the real time cost of an interruption is much more than the actual time your visitor spends in our office.

Learning to manage these negative interruptions takes resolve and practice. Some practical tips are:

- ◆ Set a time limit and stick to it. Say: 'I have five minutes – will that do or would you rather fix a time for later?'
- ◆ Set the stage in advance; you are very busy with a deadline in sight.
- ◆ With casual droppers-in, remain standing. If they sit down, perch on the edge of your desk.
- ◆ Meet in the other person's office – then you can determine when to leave.
- ◆ Avoid small talk when you are busy; it doubles the interruption time.
- ◆ Get the other person to the point. Don't be afraid to interrupt the interrupter, asking them what the problem is. What is the purpose of his or her call?
- ◆ Be ruthless with time but gracious with people. Give them your full attention. Listen well. Be firm but friendly

and helpful. Don't let them go away empty handed if you can avoid it.

◆ Have a clock available where visitors can see it, and don't be afraid to glance at it a few times. Explain about your next appointment; a white lie is better than a black interruption.

'The mirror will always reveal to you the number one interrupter in your life – you.'

Idea 53: Deal with your paperwork

The paperwork mountain

FOR ACTION	If you can take complete action, do so at once. If that is not possible, take action. Mark on it what action is needed, then consign it to the pending tray or file. This works electronically as well as with paper. Have an effective 'brought forward' system.
FOR INFORMATION	Read and then file, throw away or pass on duly initialled. Comment directly on the paper or track on the electronic file wherever possible.
FOR READING	This is material that does not need to be read at once. Save it for marginal time. Use the folder facility on your computer to help you file things for later.
FOR WASTE PAPER	If the paper fits into none of the above categories, consign it speedily to the wastepaper basket or computer trash facility – make sure that this is emptied regularly to keep things tidy and save valuable memory space.

Some problems if left alone will solve themselves. If someone shouts for it, you can always say that you have been studying it and then get down to work rapidly. It's a bit risky, but you can save hours tackling some tasks that may evaporate before you've done your required work. Review the drawer from time to time, and never use it to put off a task you know you should do.

A final rule: clearing your desk completely, or at least leaving it in good order, should become a habit. No good workman will ever leave his workbench strewn with blunt tools, wood shavings and pots of congealed glue at the end of the day. A clear desk is a foundation for tomorrow's work.

'Don't keep paperwork lying around. Handle it, file it or throw it away.'

Idea 54: Make use of committed time

When one has much to put into them, a day has a hundred pockets.

Friedrich Nietzsche, philosopher

Julius Caesar dictated to five secretaries who accompanied him on horseback as he rode on his campaigns – his way of making full use of committed time.

Some tips for making the best use of your committed time:

◆ You have to commit time, but not all committed time is used. Become aware of time as a piece of cloth that you are continually cutting into shape. Pick up the offcuts, the pieces of marginal time, and make use of them.

◆ Waiting time, be it long or short, can be a positive opportunity rather than a negative time drag. Become a wait watcher!

◆ Waiting time, in an airport lounge or hospital for instance, gives you some bonus minutes of solitude if not silence. Be prepared for them by having the right frame of mind. As the dramatist and philosopher Goethe once said,

> *Solitude is a wonderful thing when one is at peace with oneself and when there is a definite task to be accomplished.*

◆ When choosing the most time-effective method of travel, take into account the quality and quantity of the work you will be able to do on the journey.

In what ways can I make fruitful use of my committed time in the next month?

Follow-up test

Developing a personal sense of time

☐ Have you become fully aware of the value of your time – and other people's time?

☐ Are you clear about your chief aim?

☐ Do you now know what you should be busy about – in a word, your business?

☐ Do you allow a sufficient amount of time for quiet thought and reflection?

Major time savers

☐ Are you able to say 'no' with firmness and politeness?

☐ Have you developed your skills of delegation?

☐ Do you avoid wasting other people's time by always doing what you commit yourself to doing?

☐ 'Procrastination is the thief of time.' How much of your time is it stealing at present?

☐ How much of your time do you invest in fruitless regrets about what is now past history?

☐ Can you recall an instance when you found yourself wasting time through having made the same avoidable mistake twice?

☐ Are you a good judge of when to cut your losses?

_____

_____

Principles of planning

☐ Do you look on time planning as a skill that can be improved?

☐ Do you always consider the 'worst-case scenario'?

☐ Have you grasped the principle that time spent on careful planning saves time in the execution of the plan?

☐ Can you set clear, specific and time-bounded objectives?

_____

_____

Effective daily work

☐ Does your day just happen or do you plan your day with certain outputs or outcomes in mind?

☐ How good are you at prioritizing – identifying the key things on your agenda that are top priority?

☐ Do you manage carefully the 20 percent of your time that produces 80 percent of your productivity?

☐ Do you control interruptions or do they control you?

☐ Have you mastered the act of using committed time?

PART THREE

Developing your Leadership Skills

Leadership is a symbiotic phenomenon. You will never go out into the street and meet someone who is *just* a leader. They will be a nurse *and* leader, a teacher *and* leader, a salesperson *and* leader, a soldier *and* leader, an administrator or manager *and* leader, and so on.

It is the *vocational* nurse, teacher or salesperson who tends to become a leader, because their heart and soul are in the business. They don't lack enthusiasm, for example, that key leadership quality. If they can develop the necessary leadership skills at whatever level they aspire to reach, they will be accepted by their colleagues as natural leaders. Leadership gives them a means of adding extra value.

 Do I want to be a leader in my field?

The talent for true leadership often emerges slowly – it is a late developer. It often surprises people to discover that the quiet people who know their business often make the best leaders. So remain open to the idea that leadership may be your second talent.

Do not think of successful leadership solely in structural terms, like getting to the top of the hierarchy. You can achieve excellence in leadership at all levels and you can also exercise leadership from marginal positions. Alternatively or in addition, you may find yourself in the informal role of being a thought leader.

My focus in Part Three is on the role of leader, but you can use all the knowledge and know-how here to become a more effective team member. What matters is getting worthwhile things done; whether you are team captain or team player is a secondary issue. You should aim for personal and team success in either role.

Four Greatest Ideas on Career Management

Idea 55: From specialist to business leader

The Hourglass-shaped and the Inverted Funnel models of career change give you two broad vocational paths. Stay as a specialist and seek excellence, or widen out as a generalist, as an organizational leader. If you take the second path, excellence remains your aim, but it is now excellence as a leader.

The Hourglass-shaped and Inverted Funnel Models of Career Change

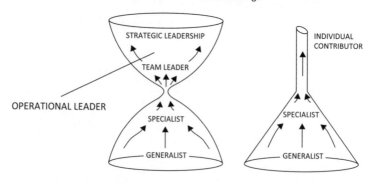

The story or process of your career can be represented as being like the shape of an hourglass or egg timer. As you move upward through the narrow neck of the glass, you begin to acquire the wider knowledge or experience of the purpose of the organization as a whole, as compared with your specialized part or contribution within it. That career movement, however, sets up the need for development in leadership, communication and decision making where you are not a technical expert.

If you take the generalist path you now have a second talent to work out – the talent of leadership.

Idea 56: Checklist: Are you a born leader yet?

☐ In the past year, has anyone used the words leader or leadership to describe you?

☐ Bearing in mind that leadership is service, do you still aspire to a leadership role?

☐ Have you read any books on leadership or attended any leadership courses?

☐ Is your temperament or personality such that you create harmony in groups rather than divisiveness?

☐ Does it come naturally to you to be interested in other people, especially in their interests and aptitudes?

☐ Have others described you as 'a good judge of character'?

☐ Do you believe that people need stimulus and encouragement if they are to persevere in the journey of discovering and using the best that lies within them?

☐ When you have been in a leadership role have you found it – in spite of the hassle – fundamentally enjoyable and personally rewarding?

Idea 57: Can leadership be developed?

You are not born a leader, you become one.

Proverb of the Bamileke people, West Africa

Yes it can.

Your progress, however, will be the interaction of three factors:

◆ *Nature* – your natural aptitude for leading others. Aptitude is a natural ability to learn and become proficient in a particular function; a natural liking for some activity and the likelihood of success in it. It suggests quickness in learning.

◆ *Study* – acquiring some of the global body of knowledge about leadership, starting with the essential principles.

◆ *Practice* – actually doing leadership over a period of time, perhaps in different fields and at different levels.

People's natural potential varies, but without study and practice it is like grapes that wither on the vine. Use it or lose it.

Exercise

Write down the five lessons about being an effective leader that experience – your combination of study and practice – has taught you.

1

2

3

4

5

You can't learn leadership out of books. What a good guidebook to the body of knowledge – I don't mean the latest theories or fads – will do for you is to help you to learn quicker from practice. You may well overtake the born leaders.

As Francis Bacon wrote long ago in *The Advancement of Learning* (1605):

> *For the wisdom of business, wherein man's life is most conversant, there be no books of it … if books were written of this experience … I doubt not but learned men with mean experience, would far excel men of long experience without learning, and outshoot them in their own bow.*

Idea 58: Awareness, understanding and skill

Leadership and learning are indispensable to each other.

J F Kennedy (from notes of a speech he was never to deliver, found in his pocket after his assassination)

To become an effective leader your top priority is to develop your:

- ◆ *Awareness* – becoming sensitive to what is happening in groups or organizations, and why it is happening; the 'group dynamics' of the situation.
- ◆ *Understanding* – knowing what leadership function or act is required at any given time.
- ◆ *Skill* – having the skill to do the function effectively in order to achieve the desired result.

Skill, from an Old Norse word, is roughly synonymous with *ability* – being able to use one's knowledge effectively in execution or performance or technical expertise.

A skill is a learned power of doing something competently. It is a *developed* aptitude or ability. It may refer, most simply, to relatively commonplace abilities gained largely through training. But it may also refer to ability that training alone could not account for without considerable natural talent, such as the skill of a prima ballerina.

In order to reach the level of skill you need to understand the nature of working groups and see clearly what is the role of the leader in teams or organizations.

Remember that you will always need to consider three variables:

- ◆ *The leader* – qualities of personality and character.
- ◆ *The situation* – partly constant, partly varying.
- ◆ *The group* – the followers: their needs and values.

Five Greatest Ideas for Understanding Groups and Organizations

Idea 59: Group personality and group needs

Working groups are more than the sum of their parts: they have a life and identity of their own. All such groups, providing they have been together for a certain amount of time, develop their own unique ethos – their *group personality*.

 How would I describe the personality of my group?

The other side of the coin concerns what groups share in common as compared with their uniqueness. They are analogous to individuals in this respect: different as they are, working groups share certain *needs*.

 What needs do I think my group has in common?

Idea 60: Task, team and individual

There are three areas of need present in all working groups and organizations. They are:

- ◆ The need to achieve the common *task*.
- ◆ The need to be held together or maintained as a *team*.
- ◆ The needs that *individuals* bring into the group by virtue of being individual and embodied human beings.

These sets of needs can be illustrated as three overlapping circles.

 Can I think of any working group that doesn't have one or more of these three areas of need?

Idea 61: Three sets of needs

Task needs

Work groups and organizations come into being because there is a task to be done that is too big for one person. You can climb a hill or a small mountain by yourself, but you cannot climb Mount Everest on your own – you need a team for that.

Team maintenance needs

Many of the written or unwritten rules of working groups are designed to promote unity and to maintain cohesiveness at all costs. Those who rock the boat or infringe group standards or the corporate balance may expect reactions varying from friendly indulgence to considerable pressure.

This need to create and promote group cohesiveness I have called the team maintenance need. After all, everyone knows what a team is.

Individual needs

Thirdly, individuals bring into the group their own needs – not only the physical ones for food and shelter (which are largely catered for by the payment of wages these days) but also the psychological ones: recognition; a sense of doing something worthwhile; status; and the deeper needs to give to and receive from other people in a working situation. These individual needs are perhaps more profound than we sometimes realize.

Exercise

1   What are the task needs of your team?

2   What are your team maintenance needs?

3   What are your individual needs?

Idea 62: The interaction of the three circles

The Three Circles model suggests quite simply that the task, team and individual needs are always interacting with each other, for good or for ill.

To understand this dynamic positive or negative interaction, think of the knock-on effects in the other two circles of any change in one circle.

For example, if a group achieves its task, that in itself will tend to draw its members closer together.

On the negative side, if a group lacks harmony and has internal communication problems, it will be less capable of effective work on the common task, as well as being less likely to meet the social need of individual members.

 Each of the circles must always be seen in relation to the other two. As a leader, you need to be continually aware of what is happening in your group in terms of the three circles.

Idea 63: Checklist – The three circles

☐ Have you been able to give specific examples from your own experience on how the three circles or areas of need – task, team and individual – interact with each other?

☐ Can you identify your natural bias:
- ◆ You tend to put the task first, and are low on team and individual.
- ◆ For you the team seems more important; you value happy relationships more than productivity or individual job satisfaction.
- ◆ Individuals are supremely important to you; you always put the individual before the task or the team, for that matter. You tend to over-identify with the individual.
- ◆ You can honestly say that you maintain a balance, and have feedback from superiors, colleagues and subordinates to prove it.

Ten Greatest Ideas for Effective Leadership

Idea 64: The generic role of leader

A picture is worth a thousand words.

Chinese proverb

Perhaps the greatest ever discovery in the field of leadership development has been the discovery of the generic role of *leader*, that which is common to all leaders in all fields, at all levels and in all cultures. Here it is, another set of three circles:

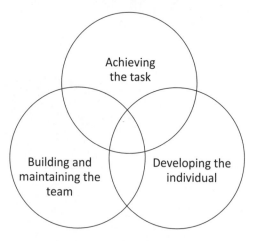

A *role* is a metaphor drawn from the theatre. It is a part played in society – in communities of purpose. Roles are immensely varied and they are largely determined by people's expectations.

 How would I describe my role as a leader, at whatever level?

Idea 65: Eight leadership functions

DEFINING THE TASK	Correctly specifies what needs to be accomplished and breaks this task down into its discrete parts.
PLANNING	Formulates an effective method for achieving the task(s), i.e. organizes people, materials, time and resources in such a way that the objective(s) can be met.
BRIEFING	Allocates tasks and resources to subordinates in such a way that each person (a) knows what is expected of him or her and (b) understands the importance of his or her contribution.
CONTROLLING	Keeps things running to plan. Is sensitive to problems and delays and is quick to respond to them. Coordinates the work of the team.
EVALUATING	Makes accurate and insightful judgments about proposals, past performance and people.
SUPPORTING	Encourages group/individuals; builds and maintains good team spirit.
MOTIVATING	Creates and maintains the team's commitment to, and interest in, the task.
SETTING AN EXAMPLE	Exemplifies the values and behaviours he/she wishes to see in others.

Idea 66: Sharing decisions

When people are of one mind and heart they can have Mount Tai.

> Chinese proverb (Mount Tai is a famous mountain in Shangdon Province, the highest known to Confucius)

It is useful for you as a leader to know the options open to you in decision making or problem solving.

Decision making continuum

| Leader makes decision and announces it | Leader 'sells' decision | Leader presents ideas and invites questions | Leader presents tentative decision subject to change | Leader presents problem, gets suggestions, makes decision | Leader defines limits; enables team to reach consensus |

The decision-making continuum is a simple model: it uses the metaphor that a decision is like a cake that can be shared in different ways between the leader and the team as a whole or any individual member. At one end of the continuum the leader has virtually all the cake: he or she issues an order or command. The next point on the line is where the leader says what is to be done but gives reasons and persuades. The remaining four points on the continuum – the different shares of the cake – are fairly self-evident.

You should always bear in mind an important general principle: the more you move to the right of the continuum the better, for the more people share in the decisions that affect their working life, the more they are motivated to carry them out. And as a leader, you are in the business of being a motivator.

Do I always seek to share decisions with others so as to gain both their wisdom and their commitment?

Idea 67: The 50:50 rule for motivation

If you know the nature of water it is easier to row a boat.

Chinese proverb

This rule says that 50 percent of our motivation comes from within us as we respond to our internal program of needs; 50 percent comes from outside ourselves, especially from the leadership we encounter in life.

The 50:50 rule is not meant to be mathematically accurate; rather, it is indicative of the ever-shifting balance between internal and external influences. From it I have deduced six key principles for leaders who want to motivate others. These are as follows:

1. *Be motivated yourself.* If you are not fully committed and enthusiastic, how can you expect others to be?
2. *Select people who are highly motivated.* It is not easy to motivate the unwilling. Choose those who have the seeds of high motivation within them.
3. *Set realistic and challenging targets.* The better the team and its individual members, the more they will respond to objectives that stretch them, provided that these are realistic.
4. *Remember that progress motivates.* If you never give people feedback on how they are progressing, you will soon demotivate them.
5. *Provide fair rewards.* This isn't easy. Do you reward the whole team, or each individual, or both? Either way, the perception of unfair rewards certainly works against motivation.
6. *Give recognition.* This costs you nothing, but praise and recognition based on performance are the oxygen of the human spirit.

When people are truly inspired, material rewards become irrelevant and the fear of punishment is totally absent.

You do not need a whip to urge on an obedient horse.
Russian proverb

Idea 68: The Adair short course on leadership

The six most important words: 'I admit I made a mistake.'
The five most important words: 'I am proud of you.'
The four most important words: 'What is your opinion?'
The three most important words: 'If you please.'
The two most important words: 'Thank you.'
The one most important word: 'We.'
The one least important word: 'I.'

Idea 69: The hallmarks of an excellent team

Hallmarks (from Goldsmiths' Hall in London, where gold and silver articles were assayed and stamped) are official marks stamped on gold and silver articles in England to attest their purity. Here are the characteristics or features that distinguish an excellent team from its copper or brass fellows:

◆ *Clear, realistic and challenging objectives* – The team is focused on what has to be done, broken down into stretching but feasible goals, both team and individual. Everyone knows what is expected of him or her.

◆ *Shared sense of purpose* – This doesn't mean that the team can recite the mission statement in unison! Purpose here is energy plus direction, what engineers call a vector. It should animate and invigorate the whole team. All share a sense of ownership and responsibility for team success.

◆ *Best use of resources* – A high-performance team means that resources are allocated for strategic reasons for the good of the whole. They are not seen as the private property of any part of the organization. Resources include people and their time, not just money and material.

◆ *Progress review* – The willingness to monitor their own progress and to generate improvements characterize excellent teams. These improvements encompass process – how we work together – as well as tasks – what we do together.

◆ *Building on experience* – A blame culture mars any team. Errors will be made, but the greatest error of all is to do nothing so as to avoid making any! A wise team learns from failure, realizing that success teaches us nothing and continual success may breed arrogance.

◆ *Mutual trust and support* – A good team trusts its members to pursue their part in the common task. Appreciation is expressed and recognition given. People play to each other's strengths and cover each other's weaknesses. The level of mutual support is high. The atmosphere is one of openness and trust.

◆ *Communication* – People listen to one another and build on one another's contributions. They communicate openly, freely and with skill (clearly, concisely, simply and tactfully). Issues, problems and weaknesses are not side-stepped. Differences of opinion are respected. Team members know when to be very supportive and sensitive, and when to challenge and be intellectually tough.

◆ *Riding out the storms* – At times of turbulent change it is never going to be all plain sailing. When unavoidable storms and crises arise, an excellent team rises to the challenge and demonstrates its sterling worth. It has resilience.

Idea 70: Leadership qualities

I cannot hear what you say, because what you are is shouting at me.

Zulu proverb

Exercise

Take some paper and make a list of the five or six qualities expected in those working in your field.

Check your list out with your colleagues.

Having done this exercise many times – for example with production workers, sales staff, nurses, engineers and accountants – I don't expect you to find it too difficult. Notice that words may vary – 'hard-working' and 'industrious', for example – but the concepts of the traits, qualities or abilities remain the same.

These qualities are necessary for you to be a leader, but they are not in themselves sufficient to make you be seen as one. For example, you cannot be a military leader without physical courage. But there are plenty of soldiers with physical courage who are not leaders – it is a military virtue. So what other qualities do you need?

Generic leadership traits

You will have noticed that the leadership qualities you have identified are very much anchored in your particular field. There may well be some commonality, but certainly the degrees to which the qualities are required will vary considerably. There are, however, some more generic or transferable leadership qualities that you should recognize in yourself – you will certainly see them in other leaders.

The qualities of leadership across the board are:

- ◆ *Enthusiasm.* Can you think of any leader who lacks enthusiasm? It is very hard to do so, isn't it?
- ◆ *Integrity.* This is the quality that makes people trust you. And trust is essential in all human relationships – professional or private. 'Integrity' means both personal wholeness and adherence to values outside yourself, especially goodness and truth.
- ◆ *Toughness.* Leaders are often demanding people, uncomfortable to have around because their standards are high. They are resilient and tenacious. Leaders aim to be respected, but not necessarily popular.
- ◆ *Fairness.* Effective leaders treat individuals differently but equally. They do not have favourites. They are impartial in giving rewards and penalties for performance.
- ◆ *Warmth.* Cold fish do not make good leaders. Leadership involves your heart as well as your mind. Loving what you are doing and caring for people are equally essential.
- ◆ *Humility.* This is an odd quality, but characteristic of the very best leaders. The opposite of humility is arrogance. Who wants to work for an arrogant manager? The signs of a good leader are a willingness to listen and a lack of an overweening ego.
- ◆ *Confidence.* Confidence is essential. People will sense whether or not you have it. So developing self-confidence is always the preliminary to becoming a leader. But don't let it become over-confidence, the first station on the rack leading to arrogance.

Your position never gives you the right to command. It only imposes on you the duty of so living your life that others can receive your orders without being humiliated.

Dag Hammarskjöld, former Secretary General of the United Nations

Idea 71: What leaders need to know

'You have that in your countenance which I would fain call master.'

'What is that?'

'Authority.'

Shakespeare, *King Lear*

There are broadly three kinds of authority at work:

1   The authority of *position* – job title, badges of rank, appointment.
2   The authority of *knowledge* – technical, professional.
3   The authority of *personality* – the natural qualities of influence.

Perhaps we can add now a fourth kind of authority – *moral* authority. That goes to leaders who suffer the dangers, tribulations and hardships of their people and for their people. It is the personal authority to ask others to make sacrifices.

Because he had endured years of imprisonment, Nelson Mandela acquired the moral authority to ask his fellow countrymen and women to accept difficulties and hardships on the long road to national unity and prosperity.

The authority of knowledge

Why do sailors do what the captain orders when the ship is tossed to and fro in a storm? Because they sense that the captain has knowledge of the sea and navigation, deepened by experience of many other storms. Knowledge creates confidence in others.

For this reason, your acquisition of technical and professional knowledge is actually part of your development as a leader. You are equipping yourself with one essential ingredient.

In 1940, Winston Churchill was the only cabinet minister with experience as a war minister in the First World War, quite apart from his own background as a professionally trained officer who, as a regimental commander, had briefly served on the Western Front. Apart from his gifts of oratory and character, Churchill had a considerable amount of knowledge relevant to running a war – more than his colleagues. And as the proverb says:

> *In the country of the blind, the one-eyed man is king.*

Know your field of activity

Another quality common to leaders is their willingness to work hard, to prepare themselves, to know their field of activity thoroughly. I have often heard it said of some individual: 'Oh, he'll get by on his personality.' Well, he may 'get by' for a time but if a charming personality is all he has, the day will come when he will find himself looking for a job.

I never knew President Roosevelt as well as I did some of the other world leaders, but in the few conferences I had with him I was impressed, not only by his inspirational qualities but by his amazing grasp of the whole complex war effort. He could discuss strategy on equal terms with his generals and admirals. His knowledge of the geography of the war theatres was so encyclopaedic that the most obscure places in faraway countries were always accurately sited on his mental map. President Roosevelt possessed personality, but as his nation's leader in a global conflict, he also did his homework – thoroughly.

Dwight D Eisenhower

'Authority flows to the one who knows.'

Idea 72: Levels of leadership

Ducere est servire *(To lead is to serve)*
Motto of Britain's Chartered Institute of Management

In all organizations there are three broad levels of leadership:

1. *Team* – leading a team or small group of about five to fifteen or sixteen people.
2. *Operational* – leading a significant part of the business with more than one team leader reporting to you.
3. *Strategic* – leading the whole organization.

The same generic role of leader – symbolized by the Three Circles model – is present at each level. What differs with level is *complexity*. For example, planning is relatively simple at team level compared with the kind of strategic planning that the chief executive officer of a large organization needs to deliver.

'An institution is the lengthened shadow of one man,' wrote American essayist Ralph Waldo Emerson. It used to be assumed that all that was needed for success was a great strategic leader. This is not true. What all organizations need is excellence of leadership at *all* levels – team, operational and strategic – and good teamwork between the levels of responsibility.

What is my present level of leadership?
To which level of leadership do I aspire?

Idea 73: Successful chief executives

Exercise: Have you got what it takes for a top job in leadership?

Place the following attributes in order of their value at the top level of leadership by placing a number from 1 to 25 beside them, 1 indicating the most valuable. This exercise can be done by you individually, or with others in a group.

___ Ambition

___ Willingness to work hard

___ Enterprise

___ Astuteness

___ Ability to 'stick to it'

___ Capacity for lucid writing

___ Imagination

___ Ability to spot opportunities

___ Understanding of others

___ Skill with numbers

___ Capacity for abstract thought

___ Integrity

___ Ability to administer efficiently

___ Enthusiasm

___ Capacity to speak lucidly

___ Single-mindedness

___ Willingness to work long hours

___ Willingness to take risks

___ Leadership

___ Ability to take decisions

___ Analytical ability

___ Ability to meet unpleasant situations

___ Open-mindedness

___ Ability to adapt quickly to change

___ Curiosity

Now turn to the Appendix and compare your answers with the ratings given to these attributes by a cross-section of the world's most successful chief executives.

Follow-up test

Career management

☐ There are a variety of ways in which you can become a leader in your field. Have you chosen the path or pattern that suits you best?

☐ Do you have the second talent – the aptitude to lead others in the role of team leader?

☐ Are you fully convinced now that through study and practice you can turn an aptitude to lead into an ability to lead?

☐ Do you see how you can progress from awareness to understanding, and from understanding to skill?

Understanding groups and organizations

☐ Would you agree that working groups are always unique but also have needs in common?

☐ Can you recall an example from your experience of how the three areas of task, team and individual interact with each other?

_____

_____

Effective leadership

☐ Do you now have a clear idea of the generic role of a leader?

☐ Can you use your knowledge of the eight leadership functions to become a more effective team player?

☐ 'The more that people share in decisions, the more they are committed to carry them out.' Do you apply this principle in all your relations with other people?

☐ Can you think of three ways of applying the 50:50 rule for motivation in your own working life?

☐ As a team member, can you benchmark your present team against the eight hallmarks of a high-performance team?

☐ Do you recognize the importance of both the representative and the generic qualities of leadership?

☐ 'Authority flows to the one who knows.' Are you acquiring the authority of knowledge in your chosen field?

☐ If leadership is your second vocation, have you determined realistically at what level – team, operational or strategic – you can make your finest contribution?

PART FOUR

Sharpening Up Your Communication Skills

We cannot live only for ourselves. A thousand fibres connect us with our fellow men; and among these fibres, as sympathetic threads, our actions run as causes, and they come back to us as effects.

Herman Melville, author of *Moby Dick*

Communication is the lifeblood of all personal relations, both in business and the private sphere. Like time management, here is a school from which you will never graduate; there is always room for improving your communication skills.

People who enjoy a measure of personal success are usually good communicators. Nature equips us with our innate aptitude to learn a language, that unique gift that human beings enjoy and that enables us to be persons, not mere animals. Without the richness of communication that language brings, would we be human?

The theme of Part Four brings us back to one of the central pillars of my message, namely that personal success depends as much as anything else on getting on well with people.

Communication, then, is not just a matter of being able to speak effectively or write well, to chair meetings or conduct interviews. It calls for the skill of empathy.

> *If there is any one secret of success, it lies in the ability to get the other person's point of view and see things from that person's angle as well as your own.*
>
> Henry Ford

By good communication we build relationships of trust. It is the strength of our relationships that make it possible for us to 'speak the truth in love' to each other.

By study and practice you can acquire the kind of proficiency in the art of communication that you need if you are going to play to the full your part in the world's business.

Seven Greatest Ideas for Better Communication

Idea 74: The Communication Star model

There are six elements involved in communication, which can be expressed as a star:

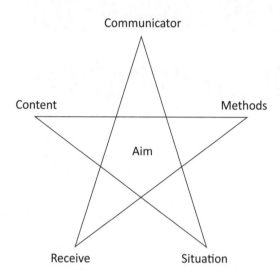

All communication is a pattern of lines or relationships between these points:

- ◆ *Communicator* – A communication in the deliberate or conscious sense implies a person(s) who sends a message.
- ◆ *Receiver* – If in the language of grammar the sender is the 'subject', then the receiver is the 'object' to whom the message is directed.
- ◆ *Aim* – The intention of the message is the purpose in the sender's mind for sending it; it is the reason communication is taking place.

◆ *Content* – The substance of the message, its component ideas, facts and less obvious value contents.

◆ *Methods* – How the message is conveyed, by writing, speaking or using signs, for example.

◆ *Situation* – The context or environment in which the communication is taking place.

Idea 75: How to use the Communication Star

- ◆ Good communication requires an understanding and skilled *communicator*, presenting a true and necessary *content* to an alert and able *communicant*, using the most appropriate *methods* in a *situation* that is contributing to the meeting of their minds, so that the *aim* is fully achieved.

- ◆ You can use the Communication Star as a practical framework when planning for any meeting. If you get it right, there should be a near-perfect harmony between the five elements in relation to the *aim*.

- ◆ Examine the true purpose of each communication. Always ask yourself what you really want to accomplish with your message.

- ◆ When it comes to content, bear in mind the enduring value of truth in any human communication. As one Ethiopian proverb says: 'Over truth there is light.'

- ◆ Consider the total physical and human setting whenever you communicate. Check your sense of *timing* against the situation. There is a time and a place for everything.

- ◆ Take the opportunity, when it arises, to convey something of help or value to the receiver.

- ◆ Be sure that your actions support your communication. Words should interpret what is done and action should accompany words. Eventually our words should become acts and our acts our truest words.

- ◆ Seek not only to be understood but also to understand – be a good listener.

Truth has such a face and such a mien,
As to beloved needs only to be seen.

John Dryden, *The Hind and the Panther* (1687)

Idea 76: Non-verbal communication

Communication is the art of being understood.

Peter Ustinov, British actor and dramatist

The concept of communication embraces a wide range of meanings that circle around the idea of *sharing*. That sharing or exchange is now more commonly related to abstract things, notably meaning.

For communication to happen, there are some necessary elements or conditions: social contact, a common medium, transmission and understanding.

Some contact or connection is required. It may be physically close or, through technology, at a distance. If you are out of touch with people you can't communicate with them. But you may be out of touch because you don't communicate! Communication creates relationships; relationships produce communication.

Although we have evolved language as our principal medium for communicating with each other, we retain non-verbal communication — just as a sailing yacht might have an auxiliary motor. It is especially important as both an expression of a relationship and as a means of building that relationship. In Japan, as in African tribal society, for example, how near or far you sit from the door indicates your seniority.

 Am I sufficiently aware of non-verbal communication as an indicator of an underlying relationship?

Idea 77: Six rules for effective public speaking

Use what language you will, you can never say anything but what you are.

Ralph Waldo Emerson

Public speaking – the art or power of communicating or expressing thought through the spoken word – takes many different forms, ranging from the formal – addresses, discourses, orations, lectures, homilies, sermons, presentations – to the less formal. These six rules apply to them all. Apply them and you will, with practice, become an effective speaker.

1   *Be clear* and make your communication unclouded or transparent. A clear sky is one free of clouds, mists and haze. With reference to speech it means free of any confusion and hence easy to understand. Being clear is not primarily a matter of sentences and words. The value of clarity is an inner one: it should act as a principle, purifying thought at its source, in the mind.

2   *Be prepared* means active, conscious deliberation and effort before action. To be unprepared, by contrast, means that you have not thought or made any attempt at readying yourself for what you know you may or will have to face. You are like a soccer team that never trains or plans before its matches.

3   *Be simple*, so that your hearers are not put off by anything unnecessarily complicated or intricate. But don't over-simplify or talk down to your audience – even if they are children.

4   *Be vivid* – make it come alive! This graphic or colourful quality springs from the interest and enthusiasm in the

mind and heart of the communicator, but it has to become visible in your language.

5   *Be natural* or, if you prefer it, be yourself. What you say and how you say it should reflect your own innate character. Good communication is truth through personality.

6   *Be concise* – be economical with your words and other people's time. Less is more.

'The more you say, the less people remember.'

Idea 78: The art of listening

The most important thing in communication is hearing what is not said.

Peter Drucker

Listening is not the same as hearing. It is the positive business of paying heed or giving your thoughtful attention to someone while they are speaking.

The benefits of becoming a good listener include information and ideas that could be profitable to you, helping other people by lending them your ear, and deepening in the other person the desire to listen to you.

As one Ghanaian proverb says:

No one is without knowledge except he who asks no questions.

The first step to self-improvement is to raise your level of awareness of poor or bad listening. The symptoms of the 'disease of not listening' include irrational selectivity, irritating interruptions, switching off, mental laziness, succumbing to external distractions, and getting hung up on the speaker's voice or manner.

Readiness to listen comes first on the list of what you need for this journey. Hearing the message clearly comes next, closely followed by the work of sifting and interpretation. That may lead to further evaluation of its content and import. You should feel responsible for giving some feedback in a conscious way, so that the speaker knows if the message has been received and understood. Whether or not it further engages your interest – or will later – is another matter.

The will to listen – wanting to listen – comes first. In most contexts listening also requires an openness of mind, a willingness in principle to think or act differently.

Listening – or at least very good listening – demands the whole of your mind and heart. That is why the challenge to become an excellent listener is such an exciting one. Not all of us may become great speakers, but great listening is within our grasp.

> *'Listen first, speak last.'*

Idea 79: Accentuate the positives

In almost any form of communication – meetings, interviews, public speaking – it is good policy always to start with something positive. It might be a short thanks or repeating the obvious, but it really can smooth the way for results. A negative start always produces a negative response.

Bear this principle in mind if it falls to your lot to offer critical feedback – or constructive advice – to others.

You and I are not the greatest people alive, I know, but we aren't completely useless: there are some positive things about us. Avoid like the plague those people who are colour blind to the positives in you. They only see the negatives, the shades of gray. They have nothing to contribute to you. They are drains, not radiators.

Try to find three positives to start off on and additionally, if you do give blunt feedback that might be considered negative, have a few solutions or creative answers in your back pocket to pull out to encourage others.

Idea 80: Make the best use of feedback

When a man says you are a horse laugh at him. When two men assert that you are a horse, give it a thought. And when three men say you are a horse, you had better go and buy a saddle for yourself.

Hungarian folk saying

Feedback is a term from electronics, for the phenomenon where some of an output returns to the sender in the form of an input. In our social life praise is a common form of it.

Not all feedback is as pleasing or as welcome as praise. On the other hand, you seldom learn anything when others praise you. Critical feedback can be sharper, especially for those short on humility, but it is definitely more instructive.

Remember that all that your critic is doing is giving you their *impression* of you. If you can discern a pattern in the feedback you receive, then that enhances its value. Use your judgment. Remember that any form of truth about yourself – about how you are coming over to others – is valuable. It gives you options, for it is well within your power to change your attitude.

In receiving constructive criticism you should:

- ◆ Remain quiet and listen.
- ◆ Not find fault with the criticizing person.
- ◆ Try not to manipulate your appraiser by taking up the emotional role of a victim.
- ◆ Try not to change the subject.
- ◆ Not caricature the complaint.
- ◆ Not ascribe an ulterior motive to the appraiser.
- ◆ Give the impression that you understand the point.

In the face of any kind of criticism you should be open to it and not instinctively ignore, deny or deflect it. Whether or not you accept all or part of it is a secondary issue.

 When given feedback, do I always try to grasp the point in its fullness before accepting or rejecting it?

Five Greatest Ideas for Productive Meetings

Idea 81: Five types of meeting

A briefing meeting

A briefing meeting is called by the manager to direct or instruct his or her team members to undertake a particular task or to lay down policy governing future conduct. It is characterized by:

- ◆ Giving instructions and information.
- ◆ Clearing up misunderstandings.
- ◆ Integrating ideas and views where appropriate.

An advisory meeting

An advisory meeting is called essentially for the exchange of information. It is not a decision-making meeting as such. It is characterized by:

- ◆ Seeking advice about a problem.
- ◆ Informing others about ideas.
- ◆ Listening to views.

A council meeting

A council meeting is held between people of equal standing who have some professional knowledge or skill to contribute to the matter in hand. It is characterized by:

- ◆ Decisions being made by consensus.
- ◆ Accountability lying with the group.
- ◆ Resolving differences by talking them through.

A committee meeting

A committee meeting is one in which representatives from various groups or interests meet on a roughly equal footing to make decisions on matters of common concern. It is characterized by:

- ◆ A sense of authority.
- ◆ Differences ultimately being resolved by voting.
- ◆ Compromises being common.

A negotiating meeting

A negotiating meeting is also one in which representatives of different interests meet, but decisions are made more on a bargaining basis than by voting. It is characterized by:

- ◆ Decisions being taken on a *quid pro quo* basis.
- ◆ Each side having different but overlapping aims.
- ◆ Each side seeking to achieve the best terms for itself.

> *'Nothing is impossible until it is sent to a committee.'*

Idea 82: Managing meetings

Meetings are an inescapable part of corporate or social enterprise. Resolve to run them in a time-effective way. Begin by distinguishing between the five different kinds or purposes of meeting (Idea 81).

Becoming more cost-conscious about meetings will help you to be economical with time. Check if any given meeting is really necessary and ensure that people don't waste their time attending meetings if their presence is not required.

Time spent on planning the meeting will repay itself tenfold. Work out the agenda carefully, allotting time for each item.

Clear, concise and definite minutes are necessary. Although not always essential, they should normally make reference to who is to do what by when and with a deadline time for reporting back.

> *It is essential for the Cabinet to move in, leaving in its wake a trail of clear, crisp, uncompromising decisions. That is what government is about. And the challenge to democracy is to get it done quickly.*
>
> Clement Attlee, former UK prime minister

Idea 83: Be prepared

 Is this meeting really necessary?

Careful preparation is the secret of productive meetings. First and foremost, it is essential that the chair be clear about the objective or objectives of the proposed meeting. A useful way of double-checking is to ask yourself: 'Where should we all be at the end of this meeting?'

There are four practical steps for meeting preparation:

1   *Determine the purpose of the meeting*

Consider possible aims, such as:

- ◆ To engage in joint consultation.
- ◆ To develop support for action.
- ◆ To resolve unsolved problems.

2   *Explore the subject*

- ◆ Collect/research facts and information.
- ◆ Identify the main topics to be discussed.
- ◆ Consider probable differences in viewpoint.

3   *Outline the discussion*

- ◆ Set the final objective.
- ◆ Consider intermediate objectives.

◆ Frame questions to develop discussion.
◆ Plan the introduction especially, and include the main topics for discussion.
◆ Prepare a timetable for the meeting.

4   *Have everything ready*

◆ Issue invitations and information in good time.
◆ Arrange accommodation.
◆ Prepare necessary materials, include aids such as flip-charts or digital presentations.

Idea 84: Six golden rules for the chair

Making meetings effective

	START ON TIME
AIM	**OUTLINE PURPOSE CLEARLY**
	State problems/situation/reason
	Define constraints and limitations
	Establish task(s) of meeting
GUIDE	**ENSURE EFFECTIVE DISCUSSION**
	Introduce topic(s) for discussion
	Draw out opinions, viewpoints and experiences
	Develop group interest and involvement
	Keep discussion within staged task(s)
CRYSTALLIZE	**ESTABLISH CONCLUSIONS**
	Recognize degrees of feeling and changes of opinion
	Summarize points of agreement and disagreement
	State intermediate conclusions as they are reached
	Check understanding and acceptance
ACT	**GAIN ACCEPTANCE AND COMMITMENT**
	Summarize and state conclusion(s) clearly
	Gain commitment to action plan
	State responsibility for action
	Make sure that everybody understands
	END ON TIME

Then do what you are committed to do. Make it happen.

Idea 85: Always follow up with action points

Good follow-up is just as important as the meeting itself. Peter Drucker and I once discussed this very point over a working lunch on strategic leadership. Peter instanced Alfred Sloan as an exemplar of best practice. Sloan, who headed General Motors from the 1920s until the 1950s, was, he told me, 'the most effective business executive I have known'.

Sloan announced the purpose at the beginning of a formal meeting. Then he listened. He rarely spoke except to clarify a misunderstanding and never took notes. He summed up at the end, thanked the participants and left. Immediately afterward he wrote a short memo to all attendees summarizing the discussion and its conclusions, listing the work assignments decided on in the meeting. He specified the executive who was to be accountable and the deadline for completion.

'Any given meeting is either productive or a total waste of time.'

Follow-up test

Better communication

☐ Can you think of any field of work where the ability to communicate well with others does not contribute to personal success?

☐ Do you work on the principle that communication is essentially two-way rather than one-way?

☐ When planning a communication event, do you give full consideration to all the six points of the Communication Star model?

☐ Are you fully aware of the importance of non-verbal communication in expressing and building relationships?

☐ When you speak at meetings of any kind, do you consciously seek to apply the six principles for effective public speaking?

☐ Have you set your sights on becoming a master in the art of listening?

☐ When communicating with others, do you always try to 'accentuate the positives'?

☐ Can you heed, sift and use the constructive elements in the feedback that comes your way?

Productive meetings

☐ Are you aware that the meetings you attend fall into five main types, depending on their purpose?

☐ Do you plan sufficiently to make the meetings you attend productive?

☐ Do the meetings you arrange invariably start on time and end on time?

☐ Are you noted for being able to lead meetings effectively?

☐ Have you developed a system for ensuring that action follows discussion, decision and commitment?

PART FIVE

Effective
Thinking Skills

*The 'untrapped mind' is open enough to see many possibilities,
humble enough to learn from anyone and everything, perceptive enough to see things as they really are, and wise enough
to judge their true value.*

Konusuke Matsushita

The importance of having an 'untrapped mind', as Matsushita calls
it, should be self-evident for anyone who is on a journey that aspires
to success in one's profession. Apart from good judgment in your
chosen field, you need to develop the more generic thinking skills
listed and described in Part Five.

Behind decision making and problem solving lies your ability as a practical thinker. Learning how to use your mind – *all* of your mind, including your depth or unconscious mind – is both productive and fun.

Your depth mind, as I call the unconscious part of the brain – nature's personal computer – plays a major part in creative or innovative thinking. It is the source of ideas. Many a success story is built on the foundation of just one really good idea – and it doesn't always have to be an original one.

Extend your creativity to the core business of using and developing your talents to the full for the good of others. Creativity and a creative attitude to life aren't just for the privileged few – they're your birthright.

Thought is not a trick, or an exercise, or a set of dodges. Thought is a man in his wholeness wholly attending.

D.H. Lawrence

Fifteen Greatest Ideas for Effective Thinking Skills

Idea 86: Knowing your mind

When your mind is thinking to some purpose, there are three meta-functions or families of mental skills at play: analyzing, synthesizing and valuing:

- ◆ *Analyzing* is essentially separating, dissecting or taking things apart to see what they are made of.
- ◆ *Synthesizing* is essentially putting things together, assembling, joining up.
- ◆ *Valuing* is essentially assessing the worth of something according to some scale of reference.

When we think we are continually switching from one 'musical key' of thinking to another, though we are seldom aware of doing so.

The human mind can think purposively on different levels of consciousness. Quite a lot of analyzing, synthesizing and valuing is done at a subliminal or less than conscious level. I call this the depth mind. It is especially associated with memory, intuition and creativity.

Emotion or feeling can encourage and fuel effective thinking, but negative emotions – fear in all its forms – have mostly bad effects. As a leader you need to be in complete command of yourself to ensure that negativity doesn't take over.

Knowledge of the range, depth and capability of your own mind gives you knowledge of all other human minds, not least those of your colleagues at work.

Idea 87: Clear thinking

I keep six honest serving-men,
They taught me all I knew.
Their names are What and Why and When
And How and Where and Who.

Rudyard Kipling

To improve your decision-making capability you need to become a clear thinker. Can you call to mind three people you have met who had or have a reputation for their clear thinking?

The way to improve your skills as a clear thinker is to challenge all that appears to be – in your own thinking or in the thoughts of others – sloppy, inconclusive, blurred, confused, doubtful, foggy, fuzzy, muddled, obscure, unclear, unintelligible or vague. You won't be short of work!

There is a link between having a good analytical mind and being a clear thinker. You have to be able to reduce a complex problem or situation to its essentials. Questions play a key in clear thinking. Indeed, sometimes finding the right question to ask is more important than anything else at the time.

What you need is the ability to think for yourself, as if from first principles. That requires a balance of confidence and humility: confidence in your own intellectual powers and humility that keeps you from that fatal form of over-confidence known as arrogance.

Beware of 'paralysis by analysis'. If a decision needs to be made, you should always identify when it has to be made. Over-analyzing situations is as bad as not giving them sufficient thought in the first place.

Idea 88: Holistic thinking

I can see the whole of it at a single glance in my mind, as if it were a beautiful painting or a handsome human being.

Mozart

An analytical mind is diametrically opposite to a holistic mind. The former separates wholes into their constituent parts. That works well with inanimate objects, with all except in the case of living beings. Then, as Wordsworth said, 'We murder to dissect.'

Knowing how to think holistically – to see the wood as well as the trees, to see the whole that is the sum of more than the constituent parts – is a key skill for an effective thinker.

Those who are good judges of people tend to have more holistic minds. People may have sets of qualities or strengths and weaknesses, but a psychological analysis of their traits seldom gives you a sense of knowing them. You are always dealing with a whole person.

A baby is a whole and a baby grows. Holistic minds, I think, tend to be attracted to growth. They like to help individuals and teams, organizations and communities, even nations, to grow to their full potential.

Are you holistically minded? There is a simple test. If you are trying to understand a complex social situation, do you prefer someone to analyze it for you? Or is the gateway of understanding for you the story of how the situation developed? Holistic people like to know the story behind a person or situation.

'The most original person is the one who borrows from the most success.'

Idea 89: Imaginative thinking

A man may prophesy,
With a near aim, of the main chance of things
As yet not come to life, which in their seeds
And weak beginnings, lie intreasured.

William Shakespeare, *Henry IV*

Imagination is our power to form images in our minds or to picture or conceive things that we cannot actually see and have not directly experienced.

Imagination is also linked to the higher creative faculty. Here it creates new forms of reality, giving shape to things unknown or new by recombining the products of past experience.

Creativity is about having new ideas and innovation is about turning them into improved or new products and services. Both creativity and innovation call for imaginative thinking.

It is imagination that is needed to anticipate events and to respond to change.

Only those with a lively imagination can really develop sensitive understanding and empathy for others, be they team members, colleagues or customers.

Vision is the art of seeing things invisible.

Jonathan Swift

Idea 90: Checklist – How imaginative are you?

☐ Can you recall visually with great accuracy? Imagine your last holiday and see how much detail you can see in the mental pictures.

☐ Would you describe yourself as good at visualizing things you haven't directly experienced yourself? Could you, for example, imagine accurately what it would be like to be a member of the opposite sex? Or prime minister?

☐ Has anyone commended you for your imagination within the last year?

☐ Have you invented or made anything recently, at work or in your leisure time, that definitely required imagination?

☐ Do you tend to foresee accurately what happens before the event?

☐ Do you day-dream about your work or career?

☐ Do you paint or draw?

☐ Do you find it easy to choose colour schemes when you have to redecorate your room?

☐ Do you find that you can think up names for such things as babies, pets, houses?

☐ Have you ever written a story or poem?

Idea 91: Valuing

> *Thought is the testing of statements*
> *in the touchstone of conscience,*
> *Thought is gazing onto the face of life,*
> *and reading what can be read,*
> *Thought is pondering over experience,*
> *and coming to conclusion.*
>
> D H Lawrence

According to an ancient Roman proverb:

> *Integrity is the noblest possession.*

Integrity implies trustworthiness and incorruptibility to a degree that one is incapable of being false. A person of integrity prizes truth above all else.

Establishing the truth – the realities of the situation or what is in fact the case – is always a necessary condition for effective decision making. Not that it is easy. Indeed, in some situations truth may be hard to come by.

When making decisions we often need to consult specialists with the necessary professional or technical knowledge. But it is not wise to accept what they say without question. Here is another use of your valuing skills: you need to evaluate the advice you are given by a specialist in relation to the decision in question.

You can see now that your ability as a decision maker depends largely on your judgment, and judgment in turn is mainly a function of your values and your valuing skills.

Truth is not just factual accuracy – reflecting reality – although that remains important. It also means trustworthiness, reliability and straightforwardness.

Truth is the language that identifies what is universal.

Antoine de St. Exupery

Idea 92: Your depth mind at work

The functions of the conscious mind – analyzing, synthesizing and valuing – can also take place on a deeper level. Your depth mind can dissect for you, just as your stomach juices can break down food into its elements.

The depth mind, for example, is capable of analyzing data that you may not have known you had taken in, and comparing it with what is filed away in your memory bank. It is also capable of more than analysis. It is also close to the seat of your memory and the repository of your values. It is also a workshop where creative synthesis can be made as if by an 'inscrutable workmanship'.

An organic analogy for its function is the womb, where after conception a baby is formed and grows from living matter.

You may also have experienced the value of thinking of the depth mind's neighbour we call conscience, in the form of guilt feelings or even remorse. Conscience is useful because its red light may tell you that your decision making has led to a wrong move.

> *Dust as we are, the immortal spirit grows*
> *Like harmony in music; there is a dark*
> *Inscrutable workmanship that reconciles*
> *Discordant elements, makes them cling together*
> *In one society.*
>
> William Wordsworth

Idea 93: Intuition

Intuition is the power or faculty of immediately apprehending that something is the case. It seems to occur without any conscious reasoning.

There is plenty of evidence that effective decision makers do listen to their intuition.

Where strong emotions are in play, intuition can be highly unreliable. Equally, physical states such as tiredness or stress can distort the mind's natural workings. But in general, decision making in such low states or conditions of mind should, if possible, be avoided.

Instinct, flair and intuition are cut from the same cloth. Flair is an instinctive power of discernment in a certain field. You can 'smell' an opportunity or the direction of the path to success.

At its best, intuition works because more information is going into your mind through your senses than your faculties at a conscious level can process. So your depth mind does some informal analyzing, synthesizing and valuing, and an intuition that occurs in the conscious mind is one of its products.

If an intuition comes to you after a longish period of time it is likely to be more reliable; if it comes very early in the story, take your time in checking it out.

While the fisher sleeps the net takes the fish.

Ancient Greek proverb

Idea 94: It does get easier

If I have any advice to pass on, it is this: if one wants to be successful, one must think until it hurts. One must worry a problem in one's mind until it seems there cannot be another aspect of it that hasn't been considered. Believe me, that is hard work and, from my close observation, I can say that there are few people indeed who are prepared to perform this arduous and tiring work.

But let me go further and assure you of this: while, in the early stages, it is hard work and one must accept it as such, later one will find that it is not so difficult, the thinking apparatus has become trained; it is trained even to do some of the thinking subconsciously. The pressure that one had to use on one's poor brain in the early stages no longer is necessary; the hard grind is rarely needed; one's mental computer arrives at decisions instantly or during a period when the brain seems to be resting. It is only the rare and most complex problems that require the hard toll of protracted mental effort.

Roy Thompson, *After I was Sixty* (1975)

Idea 95: Evaluating your options

In the beginner's mind there are many possibilities, but in the expert's mind there are few.

Shunryu Suzuki

Effective decision-making has these six phases:

1 Defining the objective.
2 Gathering sufficient information.
3 Identifying the feasible options.
4 Evaluating the options.
5 Making the decision (choosing an option).
6 Testing its implementation: by feel, by measurement and by assessment.

Evaluating the options is often the most difficult part.

Notice the word *options* rather than *alternatives*. An alternative is literally one of two courses open. Decision makers who lack skill tend to jump far too quickly to the either–or alternatives. They do not give enough time and mental energy to generating at least three or four possibilities.

You need to open your mind into wide focus to consider all possibilities, and that is where creative thinking comes in. But then your valuing faculty must come into play to identify the feasible options – the ones that may or can be done, the practicable ones.

When considering your options, remember that it tends to be easier to discard an option rather than to choose it. In other words, we are often better at knowing what we don't want to do rather than what we do want to do.

You should also keep asking yourself whether or not you are over-looking some feasible course of action, perhaps because it is just too obvious. Always check your assumptions. The less hidden they are, the better.

As a general principle, if you accumulate enough information you may not need to make a conscious decision. For the decision will, as it were, be made for you. If there is no other feasible alternative, it is comparatively easy to make up your mind what to do.

> *When your enemy has only two options open him you can be sure that he will choose the third.*
>
> Otto von Bismarck, German statesman

Idea 96: How to be more creative

Creative thinking cannot be forced. If you are working on a problem and getting nowhere, it is often best to leave it for a while and let your subconscious mind take over.

Many people are still not even aware that their depth minds can carry out important mental functions for them, such as synthesizing parts into new wholes or establishing new connections while they are engaged in other activities.

Imagine your mind is like an email inbox. It would be great if you could sit down for an hour each morning before breakfast and receive inspired emails from your depth mind. But it isn't like that. The inbox might start receiving messages at any time of the day or night.

The whole creative thinking process can be described like this:

- ◆ *Preparation* – the hard work. You have to collect and sort the relevant information, analyze the problem as thoroughly as you can, and explore possible solutions.
- ◆ *Incubation* – the depth mind phase. Mental work – analyzing, synthesizing and valuing – continues on the problem in our subconscious mind. The parts of the problem separate and new combinations occur. These may involve other ingredients stored away in your memory.
- ◆ *Insight* – the 'Eureka' moment. A new idea emerges into your conscious mind, either gradually or suddenly like a fish flashing out of the water. These moments often occur when you are not thinking about the problem but are in a relaxed frame of mind.
- ◆ *Validation* – where your valuing faculty comes into play. A new idea, insight, intuition.

Idea 97: The Nine Dots test

How good are you as a creative thinker? Do you have an open mind? Are you flexible and resourceful? You may like to test yourself by tackling the following exercise.

Exercise

Take a piece of paper larger than this page and put on it a pattern of nine dots, like this:

Now connect up the dots by four straight consecutive lines (that is, without taking your pen or pencil off the paper). You should be able to complete the task within two minutes.

Turn to the Appendix for the solution.

Idea 98: Checklist – Are you thinking creatively?

- ☐ Would you describe yourself in implementing your general plans? Can you give two instances?
- ☐ How did you get on with the Nine Dots problem?
- ☐ Are you good at thinking 'outside the box' when it comes to occupational choices?
- ☐ Has anyone described you as creative and willing to take calculated risks in your career?
- ☐ Do you think that now, having reflected on this book, you will be able to fulfill your present role or position in a more creative way?
- ☐ Are you doing something in the present to help create an expanding future?
- ☐ Have you ever identified and responded to new needs for services or products caused by change?
- ☐ Do you welcome the kaleidoscope of change because it brings new opportunities and challenges to your creative spirit?

Idea 99: Useful originality

To create is always to do something new.

Martin Luther, German theologian

New ideas are essential to all human enterprise. Creativity is about having new and valuable ideas; innovation is about bringing them to market in the form of improved or new products and services.

Making analogies is often the trigger for new ideas. Creative thinking often begins with the perception of a relation – a spark of meaning – between two apparently unrelated things or ideas.

Really creative people have a wide span of relevance: they look far afield, even to remote places or times in history, for solutions to the problems they face.

It is important to think sideways, or laterally, because the seeds of a solution to a problem may lie outside the box you are working in.

The sideways thinking involved often leads to a reversal of what appears to be the natural or logical way of doing things. For example, the earliest method of making cars involved teams of men moving from one car to another. Henry Ford turned it all upside down. He put the car frames on belts and moved them past the men – the birth of the assembly line.

When you work with others in your business, foster an ethos, climate or culture that breeds useful originality.

Mankind is pre-eminently creative, destined to strive consciously for a purpose and to engage in making – that is, incessantly and eternally to make new roads, wherever they may lead.

Fyodor Dostoevsky, Russian novelist

Idea 100: Developing your thinking skills

The development of general ability for independent thinking and judgement should always be placed foremost, not the acquisition of special knowledge.

Albert Einstein

'I love thinking', wrote the science fiction writer Isaac Asimov, 'and writing is just thinking through your fingers.' I hope that this book has made you fall in love with clear thinking and to make you want to develop your thinking skills.

By this point in our journey together you should have a good idea of your strengths and weaknesses, your areas for improvement as a thinker. As always, the principle is to build on your strengths and starve your weaknesses.

You will get nowhere in your self-development journey without feedback. This comes from two sources: life and other people. The former comes to you in the form of the consequences – both expected and unexpected – of the decisions you make. Reflect on these experiences in the light of the principles in this book, and learn your lessons.

Take a piece of paper and write down the feedback you have received from others about you as a thinker; I mean as an applied thinker and decision maker. Is there a pattern in the comments you have received? What are your tendencies?

Who are the people who – by their example or their teachings – can help you to become more effective as a decision maker, problem solver and creative thinker? Remember, all experienced people have something to teach you, if you have a listening ear.

Humility is the quality that keeps you always open to learn more. It is a necessary condition for sustained personal success.

Follow-up test

Effective thinking skills

☐ Can you think of anyone who has achieved a degree of personal success who lacks good judgment in their business?

☐ Has anyone commented in the last year on your clarity of mind?

☐ Apart from your analytical skills, are you able also to think holistically, to see the whole wood and not just the trees?

☐ Would you describe yourself as good at visualizing things you haven't directly experienced yourself?

☐ Has anyone praised you for your imagination within the last year?

☐ Have you invented or made anything recently, at work or in your leisure time, that definitely required imagination?

☐ Do you tend to foresee accurately what happens before the event?

☐ Where possible, do you build into your plans time to 'sleep on it', so as to give your depth mind an opportunity to contribute?

☐ Do you deliberately seek to employ your depth mind to help you to:
   ◆ Analyze a complex situation?
   ◆ Restructure a problem?
   ◆ Reach value judgments?

☐ Have you experienced waking up the next morning to find that your unconscious mind has resolved some problem or made some decision for you?

☐ Do you see your depth mind as being like a personal computer? Remember the computer proverb: Garbage in, garbage out.

☐ Do you keep a notebook or pocket recorder at hand to capture fleeting or half-formed ideas?

☐ Do you think you can benefit from understanding how other people's depth minds work?

☐ Is your team noted for its creative ideas and willingness to try new ways or methods?

☐ Are you aware that you may have a set of unconscious assumptions that could be barriers to creative thinking?

☐ Do you sometimes consciously use your imagination when considering options in any given decision-making situation?

☐ 'The most original person is the one who borrows from the most sources.' Can you develop new ideas by drawing on a wide range of sources?

☐ Can you think of two individuals you know – a man and a woman – who show in their lives and business practical wisdom, that rare combination of intelligence, experience and goodness?

Appendix

The 25 attributes of top leaders and managers

A survey of successful chief executives on the attributes most valuable at top levels of management indicated the following, in order of rating:

1. Ability to take decisions.
2. Leadership.
3. Integrity.
4. Enthusiasm.
5. Imagination.
6. Willingness to work hard.
7. Analytical ability.
8. Understanding of others.
9. Ability to spot opportunities.
10. Ability to meet unpleasant situations.
11. Ability to adapt quickly to change.
12. Willingness to take risks.
13. Enterprise.
14. Capacity to speak lucidly.
15. Astuteness.
16. Ability to administer efficiently.
17. Open-mindedness.
18. Ability to 'stick to it'.
19. Willingness to work long hours.
20. Ambition.
21. Single-mindedness.
22. Capacity for lucid writing.
23. Curiosity.
24. Skill with numbers.
25. Capacity for abstract thought.

Solution to the Nine Dots test

The reason many people cannot solve this problem is that they put an unconscious or invisible framework around the dots, and try to solve the problem within it. That makes it impossible.

The invisible frame

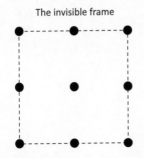

But if you break out of that self-imposed limitation, the solution to the problem is easily reached.

The solution

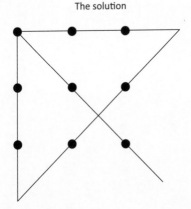

The Nine Dots test first appeared in one of my books, *Training for Decisions*, as long ago as 1969, and since then it has generated a new maxim in the English language – *think outside the box*. The 'box' in question is the unconscious framework imposed on the dots.

About John Adair

John Adair is the business guru who invented Action Centred Leadership (ACL) in the 1970s, now one of the best known leadership models in the world. Organisations worldwide use it to develop their leadership capability and management skills. ACL is being successfully applied in engineering companies, retailers, local authorities, financial institutions and universities. The British armed services base their leadership training upon it.

John's company, Adair International, provides ACL development programmes, Accredited Trainer programmes and consultancy around the world, via regional partnerships with training providers in the UK, Australia, New Zealand, the Middle East and India.

John is the author of more than 40 books, translated into many languages, and numerous articles on history, leadership and management development.

Index

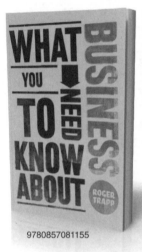